# FIFTEEN BIGGEST PROBLEMS IN EDUCATION AND HOW TO SOLVE THEM

# EDUCATION IN A COMPETITIVE AND GLOBALIZING WORLD

Additional books in this series can be found on Nova's website under the Series tab.

Additional E-books in this series can be found on Nova's website under the E-book tab.

# FIFTEEN BIGGEST PROBLEMS IN EDUCATION AND HOW TO SOLVE THEM

ILGHIZ M. SINAGATULLIN

nova publishers

*New York*

**Library of Congress Cataloging-in-Publication Data**


ISBN: 978-1-62417-599-2


*Published by Nova Science Publishers, Inc.* † *New York*

# CONTENTS

# ACKNOWLEDGEMENTS

This book has gone through many stages of development. I extend my gratitude to educators, teacher educators, school and university students on both sides of the Atlantic, who influenced my thinking and helped generate valuable ideas. I have profited from the generous aid of my colleagues from Moscow Pedagogical State University, Gertzen Russian State Pedagogical University (Saint Petersburg), Bashkir State Pedagogical University (Ufa), and Birsk State Socio-Pedagogical Academy. I acknowledge their contribution with gratitude.

I am particularly grateful to Dr. Kenneth Cushner and Dr. Linda Robertson (Kent State University) and Dr. Stephen Cary (University of San Francisco) for providing me with considerable assistance and ensuring my understanding of various aspects of American education.

I am especially grateful to Barbara Cohen (San Francisco) who has enriched my understanding of American culture and showed me a number of natural and man-made wonders in California.

I owe a great deal to Milton and Sharon Bailey, husband and wife, who took me on extensive trips, introducing me to a multicultural America.

I am thankful to the representatives of Nova Science Publishers for their support and for helping bring the project to completion.

# INTRODUCTION

The third planet from the sun is said to be located in a rather tranquil and safe place in the Milky Way, far from the galaxy's roaring center, which may be, as scientists acknowledge, a dangerous place and actually represent a black hole. The earth itself is a good place for life in general and for reasoning life in particular. It has everything for generating and sustaining life that a normal planet should have: healthful oxygen, pure water, mild atmosphere, favorable climate, fertile soil, and varied fauna and flora. Since its creation eons ago, the planet has given birth to millions of species, from tiny protozoa to huge land-dwelling carnivores and on to Homo sapiens whom we now all are. Other theories of the origin of life are many and have the right to exist, but we will leave those hypotheses for other educated adepts as a food for contemplation.

We have explored the earth and its deepest recesses and discovered oil, gas, and coal. We have discovered other planets rotating the sun and started conquering space. We have invented the television, the computer, and the mobile phone and turned the globe into a "small place." We have harnessed the powers of water by building power and atomic stations. We have built educational systems that can provide our children with values, knowledge, and skills that they need to successfully live and work in a contemporary and interdependent world.

But, in reality, the third planet from the shining celestial body is far from being an ideal place. It could have been a perfect cradle for the harmonious development of humanity and the rest of the ecosystems, but unfortunately, since recorded history, the human race that the earth houses has been experiencing cracks and numerous crises, which have been making a negative impact on all sides of life, with education as an especially vulnerable domain suffering most.

We have entered a novel stage of globalization when all, or almost all, is known about the world; when people involved in education are on the way to building the global educational space; when communication and traveling have become easy and fast; when new and unprecedented forms of digital technology, nanotechnology, and genetic engineering have emerged; when the world can be easily destroyed by the man-made powers such as nuclear, chemical, and bacteriological weapons; when the world is endangered by possible cataclysms such as global warming and ozone layer destruction; and when the world population may reach an unprecedented and staggering figure of almost 10 billion people by 2050.

In this era of globalization, not all is ideal in the business of education. Contemporary education faces a range of challenges such as the digitization of educational space; the orientation to marketable majors (market-oriented education); the orientation to life-long education; a reduced motivation for cognitive and creative activity; the emergence of English as a global language, which hugely influences all aspects of education; and the orientation on relational skills, multiple careers, and distance learning.

Throughout the world, a considerable number of teachers are overworked, underpaid, undervalued, and burned out. The teaching profession is diminished and has a low status in society. Hard working conditions, administrative pressure, and ideological and socioeconomic metamorphoses make a negative impact on teachers' nervous and immune systems. As a result, they become victims of various diseases and experience difficulty building professional careers.

The progress in computer and Internet use, upsurge of TV industry with a variety of cable and satellite channels, and thrust of speedy means of communication through email and mobile phone have immediately resulted in a regression in other spheres of human activity. Digitization of the global educational space has distracted children, adolescents, and young adults from using conventional sources of receiving information and knowledge such as textbooks, reference literature, dictionaries, and encyclopedias. Almost all schoolchildren carry in their bags, in addition to other stuff, two "invaluable" assets--a cell phone and a flash drive. Simply put, they carry a *small, "squeezed" world* about them. Hand writing of young learners has worsened owing to infrequent use of pen and paper and more time spent in seclusion by plunging into the virtual reality of the Internet and TV programs. Today, almost anything that can be found in libraries can easily be downloaded in the Internet. Technological progress has eased and facilitated one side of life and at the same time complicated other sides of it. In other words, humanity has made a tremendous step forward and, parallel to it, a considerable leap backwards leading to a whole range of negative consequences.

We, educators and parents, have a clear understanding of the fact that humanity has firmly entered the virtual world thanks to digital and satellite technologies. We understand that the virtual reality will be extending and deepening by absorbing the ever-growing information, data, and knowledge about planet earth and what is beyond it. We understand that humankind will move beyond the phenomenon of digitization and create far more advanced means of information processing and communication in the decades to come. However, with the virtual world prospering in its countless multicultural and global forms and content, a range of problems in the sphere of education still remain unsolved, unnoticed, and even ignored.

I keep meeting quite a lot of educators and people from other walks of life among different ethnic and cultural groups who are preoccupied with accentuating predominantly the positive sides of our profession, without bringing attention to the negative aspects of it. Their creed is like this: " Let us notice and think of the positive and try to get rid of bad thoughts." These educators are obviously on the right track. To tell the truth, they urge educators to be optimistically minded, and optimists are said to live longer and healthier lives. But education has its own unique laws and rules.

Like physicians, educators should first give a diagnoses and afterwards give a cure for a disease. It means that they should, in the beginning, define the degree of a student's academic development in different subject areas, and, afterwards, design and implement corresponding strategies of instruction. In fact, we should continually check and monitor each student's academic progress or regression and all the time make adjustments in the recommended tasks. Without giving the exact diagnoses or without examining, interpreting, and identifying the level of each pupil's cognitive advancement, it becomes impossible to "prescribe' an effectual suggestion or assignment. In the same manner, without defining the weak points in the system of education and the teaching profession it is difficult to recommend required remedies. The remedy should come after the correct diagnoses.

Therefore, in this book I, first, define the essence and outline of a problem and, afterwards, provide some possible remedies and recommendations of how to cure the problem. What is recommended in this book should be understood as suggestions, which should be applied prudently taking into account the place, time, and ethnocultural conditions of each class.

I explore these problems not to alarm educators, parents, and education policy makers but to challenge them revisit some of the vital issues to ameliorate pedagogical practices and systems of education. What problems do we encounter in dealing with contemporary students? What may become with the overall issues of education in the years to come? What measures should we undertake to effectively organize classroom control and help children achieve academically? How can we predict and overcome problems arising in the process of teacher-student, parent-child, and teacher-teacher interactions? Why is it important for local school district officials and governmental authorities-- responsible for the matters of education--to draw a more nurturing attention to the problems of education as the digital screen and virtual reality are sweeping the minds of young people? Why should we pay attention to building an equitable language policy in bilingual and multilingual educational settings? The author seeks to provide a range of possible explanations and answers to these and related questions.

This book is written for K-12 teachers. It may also be a good source for school principals, school district officials, and high ranking governmental officials who are involved in organizing and monitoring the issues of education and child development. People in higher echelons of power can do a lot in creating a robust pedagogical environment for educators and ameliorating the overall social and economic infrastructures in schools. In-service teachers, teacher educators as well as parents can equally benefit from getting acquainted with the book.

Even though each chapter is built to stand alone, the book represents a unified whole.

In each chapter, I discuss some problematic issues followed by a variety of suggestions and recommendations useful for classroom practice and in interacting with youngsters in school milieu and elsewhere. Each suggestion encourages educators and education policy makers with specific insights on how to deal in a corresponding situation. Obviously, no single principle, rule, or approach will work in all situations, all schools, all cultural settings, and all societies. I urge educators to look for the best that each of the presented assumptions and suggestions can offer.

### Author's note:

*In some chapters, the author cites a number of Wikipedia sources. The validity of such references has been confirmed by the author. However, the reader would be well advised that Wikipedia should be treated with caution, as the online encyclopedia is occasionally subject to error.*

*The author often illustrates theoretical assumptions with examples and case studies, in which the names of some personages have been changed.*

*Chapter 1*

# SOMETHING IS WRONG WITH EDUCATION AND THE TEACHING PROFESSION

*The sickness of the individual is intimately caused and sustained by the sickness of his civilization.*
Herbert Marcuse

*Money spent on the brain is never spent in vain.*
English proverb

Throughout ancient history, ranging from the Sumerian and Egyptian Kingdoms to the Roman Empire and Byzantium, people involved in child rearing practices did not enjoy a sufficient attention and status in human society. For example, in Rome, teachers were badly in need, but the working teachers did not earn much, which designated this profession to the bottom of social ladder (Gabucci, 2005). There is a reference that elementary teachers in Byzantium held a fairly low status in society--"hardly better than that of an artisan" (Mango, 2005, p. 125). Starting from the middle ages and up to the late 20th century, the role and status of the teaching profession was relatively high. In the contemporary, pragmatic and industrialized epoch, despite the fact that the teacher takes an active and ample part in the laborious activity of educating the young, the overall issues related to education and the teaching profession are again being unjustifiably diminished. The causal factors of why it is so are numerous; they are both external, i.e. dependent on the circumstances lying outside educators' obligations, and internal, i.e. those arising from educators' professional activity and their attitudes to the difficulties of teaching and child-rearing.

Some people place a high value on education seeing it as a vital accomplishment and a means to standing and prospects in society. In other cases, the status of being educated is relatively high only from psychological or formal perspectives. It may be high in people's hearts or, worse, only on paper. Most often, the status of education itself and of people working in the domain of education transmission to younger generations leave much to be desired.

What factors diminish the role and status of education and the teaching profession? Why does teaching take a low place on the status scale among other professions such as medicine, jurisprudence, and engineering? Being educated is not always highly esteemed among school children and teachers themselves: Whose fault is it? We shall try to provide comprehensive explanations to these and related issues.

## NEGLIGENCE OF EDUCATION, EDUCATED PEOPLE, AND ACADEMIC SCIENCE

Disinterest and indifference to education often occurs in the countries going through more pressing problems than the academic matters. Vital problems lying outside education make federal and local authorities cut estimated expenses for education, medicine and other budget-dependent spheres. In such countries, educators' salaries may be reduced to a level barely sufficient for the necessities of life. The state cannot provide neither schools and pedagogical institutions nor teachers and teacher educators. As a result, educational institutions and teachers are often advised to become self-sufficient. In such conditions, teachers feel marginalized and neglected by the state and society. Such is the case not only in the system of education but also in the state-dependent social and economic sectors, in which a sizable number of intellectual workers, disappointed with the salaries and deteriorating conditions of work, seek jobs in another country to earn more money and improve their living conditions, thus creating the infamous "brain drain" situation.

Since the mid-20th century, a strange and atypical tendency has started taking shape. Even in higher institutions where teacher education is important or central to the institutional mission, teacher education began to look like a subordinate objective. This trend may be illustrated by the California State University, which was originally a system of normal schools. These schools became comprehensive universities in the 1950s by minimizing their teacher-training function and expanding other programs, thus seeking to ameliorate their position in the hierarchy of higher education (Maher & Tetreault, 1999). This "vogue" is now taking a new turn across the Russian Federation. As the enrollments in teacher education institutions are not very high, a great number of such institutions "squeeze" and supersede teacher education programs. Instead they open programs targeted at preparing technicians, physicians, psychologists, journalists, and lawyers.

## INSUFFICIENT FUNDING

The quality of the functioning of education and related variables is largely dependent on a society's overall socioeconomic development. Education needs sufficient funding to move ahead and withstand difficulties. Most educators and teacher educators I used to interact with almost unanimously complained about experiencing a second-rate status in society. One of the main causes of this inferiority complex is low pay. Teachers may have quite a positive image and prestige in society but earning little money immediately decreases this prestige.

Receiving leftovers from national budgets, educational institutions can not afford to repair school buildings and broken equipment; replace time-worn furniture; buy necessary literature, teaching aids, computers and related technology; obtain school buses and other means of transportation; install air-conditioning; and to build sports grounds.

## FREQUENT REFORMATIONS OF THE SYSTEM OF EDUCATION

Incessant reorganizations of secondary and higher education, especially in politically and socio-economically unstable nation-states, immediately leave a mark on schools and other educational institutions, on teachers, on teacher educators, and on parents. After each successive, so-called social revolution or heated presidential/governmental election, newly emerged "rulers" and "leaders" often try to implement, along with other reforms and innovations, a wide range of changes in education. Altering educational norms, they often destroy previously well-established standards. A whole cohort of educators hardly gets used to the requirements of one educational reform when, like a bolt from the blue, a new reform comes to the agenda, bringing about a wave of severe criticism to previously established strategies and methods of education and inculcating radical changes into the living, well-functioning tissue of the system. Worse is the case when reforms are politically or ideologically motivated.

## LACK OF MOTIVATION FOR EDUCATION

Children and parents themselves often appear to be agents in diminishing the role and status of education. Practically minded children, supported by their "down-to-earth" parents, may consider education to be just a stage in life that needs passing through. Parents' pragmatic attitude towards their kids' success in school may be explained by their stoic conviction that knowledge and, ultimately, education does not sufficiently ensure success and happiness in life. Such an attitude, when passed on to their sons' and daughters', weakens the latter's aspiration for learning with wholehearted enthusiasm. Both parents and their children start looking at education and the role of teachers in their lives with precaution and prejudice.

Lack of children's motivation for learning, especially in the middle and senior classes, can also be accounted for the indifference of the state and society toward education and material success of teachers and educated people in society. Guided by such beliefs, secondary education and, quite probably, higher education may become, for a young individual, no more than a period of formal time that one needs to "patiently" pass through.

The erosion of the teaching profession, a phenomenon encompassing both secondary schools and teacher education institutions, is reflected in the psychologically unfavorable image of educators, schools, and knowledge, as well as in the low status of the educational system in general. The current unsatisfactory state in education and the teaching profession calls for expeditious action. Following are several recommendations for governments and higher officials to keep in mind:

## International Efforts

All countries should strengthen and reinforce their joint efforts and come to a unanimous consensus that education is the highest priority in human society, and not a single child, regardless of his or her ethnic, racial, language, gender, and social class background, should be deprived of the opportunity to quality education. Education and the teaching profession as its basic ingredient should be valued in every country without exception.

There should be a good international codex of laws making it incumbent upon the state and its hierarchical structures to pay a paramount attention to the issues of education. The codex must be based on democratic principles. At the same time, governments and educational systems worldwide should feel a strong responsibility and accountability for educating the younger generations and for those who take the most active part in providing these generations with knowledge, skills, values, and attitudes, that is--teachers. Teachers and teacher educators should hear, see, and feel that their occupation is cherished and supported on the *international level*. This support should be both moral and financial. Simultaneously, all this presupposes the creation of better working and living conditions for educators and the construction of better school and university buildings with all modern conveniences and equipment. International responsibility for quality education, when raised to the rank of international law, could obligate governments to considerably ameliorate their educational systems.

## National and Regional Efforts

Every nation and regional confederacy, like, for example, the European Union, should build a foundation for enhancing the role and status of education in society. The state is a tremendously multifaceted organism and possesses countless possibilities and channels to improve the current state of education, raise educators' salaries, and improve their working conditions. Governments and public at large in each country should have a transparent understanding that education is the bastion and stronghold of statehood and of all humanity.

## Priority State Investments

Education must become a priority for state investments. In some countries, the state allots just the crumbs from the master's table for the needs of education. This situation should be changed immediately. Creating favorable conditions for charity support of education and making it advantageous for contributors is an important task of state and governmental hierarchies. It would have been nice if oligarchs and businessmen could have a more profound understanding of the importance of *investing in education.*

## Long-Term Planning and Long-Term Investments

Life shows that such a step is another effective undertaking. When a state plans to invest financial resources in education for a relatively long period of time (say, 25 years ahead), the dividends are manifold. A long-term planning enables a country to change and improve the strategies of preparing its future educated and healthy citizens, provide teachers and teacher educators with necessary conditions for work and life, and to provide educational institutions with all required conveniences, teaching materials, and modern technology. Lastly, it means that the status of education and knowledge will augment in society. Under such conditions, the proceeding generations of school, college, and university students will understand the essence and meaning of what education is and why it is vital to achieve academically in school and other educational institutions.

## Mass Media Support

All media such as newspapers, radio, television, and the Internet should "shift their mentality" and support and fortify the role and status of education by all possible means. The mass media plays a considerable role in strengthening ideological and political powers. Why cannot it play a crucial role in increasing the image and prestige of education and the teacher as the central figure? Why do the means of mass media forget to highlight the families and parents who may be examples to other families in child-rearing practices?

The lion's share of what TV and radio channels transmit belong to household, gardening, fishing, hunting, and human relations topics, which, on the whole, makes a positive impact on people's lives, their professional activity, and their incentives. In this respect, I intentionally avoid mentioning erotic and pornographic material that is in great profusion in some means of mass media. One can say, "Hey, all is in its place in mass media, with thousands of channels, programs, and rubrics that satisfy the tastes of a diversity of people." In reality, not all is in its place. There is a scanty of educational channels and programs on television, radio, and the Internet. The mass media could play a tremendous role in shaping public perception about education's role in society, the importance of teacher's work in child development, and about the importance of teacher educators' work in preparing new teachers.

Throughout the world people can view various beauty contests including the annual international contest Miss Universe. In passing, it is interesting to note that, by number of the Miss Universe crown winners, the largest number of miss universes were from the United States (in 1954, 1956, 1960, 1967, 1980, 1995, and 1997); the next most successful nation is Venezuela with six winners (1979, 1981, 1986, 1996, 2008, and 2009); and then comes Puerto Rico with five finalists (1970, 1985, 1993, 2001, and 2006) ("Miss Universe," 2011). Is it not possible to organize the contests devoted to the most industrious teachers or contests in which the jury or the public at large could select the most beautiful teacher of the year? Teachers are worth such contests and, of course, worth more privileges and more national and international attention. How nice it would be if the Miss Universe Organization, which runs international beauty contests, made a concrete decision to organize *beauty contests only for educators* or contests in which educators' expertise could be measured according to certain professional standards.

It is known that much in enhancing the role of education and the status of the teaching profession depends on teachers themselves. How can they do it? I offer the following suggestions:

## Do not Lose Your Dignity

Despite external factors negatively affecting the teaching profession and diminishing its image, you are required to possess and show self-respect and reason. In each educator and in each human being, there exists an inherent worth, an absolute value that cannot be bought or sold. This entity is called *dignity*. Dignity is embedded in one's heart, but most of it is obtained. Pedagogical reality indicates that educators often obtain dignity from the "adults in their professional environment—teachers, administrators, and parents—indirectly, through their students" (McPherson, 1983, p.201).

Be more independent in your decisions. People are dependent on juridical and civil laws, definite social codes, and ideological and religious beliefs. In the context under discussion, by being independent I mean (1) not allowing one's mind to be colonized by constantly emerging and quickly waning techniques and strategies of teaching and (2) being free in conceptualizing and implementing one's own ideas in classroom and during extracurricular activities (Sinagatullin, 2009b).

Control emotions in difficult situations. Difficulties may be prompted by continual educational reforms, bureaucratic inspections, and health problems. Psychological uneasiness and tension may be entailed by the general low-status atmosphere cloaking education and the teaching profession. Dignity requires that you cope with your emotions and do not violate the required professional etiquette when working in poor conditions, overcrowded classes, and in harsh climate. Dignity presupposes that you feel good about yourself. It becomes necessary for you to respect yourself, colleagues, students and their parents and relatives. *A wise teacher can come out victorious and with dignity from any one predicament.*


## Make School a Holy Place

I have visited quite a lot of religious shrines across the world. All these visits have added an impulse of divinity into my soul and left unforgettable remembrances. I marveled at, and "inhaled" the idyllic aura of, St. Paul's Cathedral in London; the Basílica i Temple Expiatori de la Sagrada Familia (Basilica and Expiatory Church of the Holy Family) in Barcelona, Spain; the Cathedral of Our Lady of Strasbourg, France; the Cathedral of St. Basil the Blessed in Moscow; St. Isaac's Cathedral in Saint-Petersburg, Russia; the Cathedral Church of St. Peter and St. Paul in Washington; and Saint Ignatius Church and the Church of Sts. Peter and Peter in San Francisco.

Among these greatest and other temples, I was especially amazed to see St. Peter's Basilica in Rome. It is in this edifice that I involuntarily remembered a typical secondary school and envied the holiness that was reigning inside. In fact, similar holy and psychologically elevated atmosphere prevails in all religious shrines. I felt the same psychological relief in Saint Ignatius Church in San Francisco. Our schools lack such a sense of holiness and pacification.

If I marvel at the atmosphere prevailing in the interior of religious temples and churches, it does not mean that I now call upon governments to turn kindergartens and schools into religious institutions. But why cannot we turn them into *new* educational institutions that should educate *new* graduates capable of combating societal ulcers and building a *new* life? Why can we not change the general atmosphere in classrooms and school milieu for the better? Why can we not make the school a holy place too, only based on pedagogical principles? There are many "whys" that we have to solve.

## Help Your Colleagues

The teaching profession necessitates that teachers render help to each other. In my view, the successful functioning of teaching and child-rearing processes at a school depends on the collective work of the pedagogical staff and on the positive and tolerant psychological atmosphere based on the principles of mutual understanding and assistance. When a teacher is in a predicament or in a stressful mood, one of the best remedies is a colleague's aid and support (Sinagatullin, 2009b):

> A teacher is not a single-handed specialist: He or she works as a member of a team of educators. Collectively, such a team can solve a lot of problems facing an educational institution. A teacher may be of didactic help to other teachers. More experienced teachers may aid younger colleagues in unpacking some complicated theoretical ideas, implementing practical strategies of teaching, and in organizing the procedures of a lesson or extracurricular activity. Less experienced teachers may consult their older counterparts about how to solve various educational problems which constantly arise in the teaching/learning process. Teachers may help each other in solving some psychologically and pedagogically difficult dilemmas. (p. 44)

When a teacher aids a colleague, it is unwise and indecent to ask or wait for a return aid. Somewhere in the routine of school life or in a difficult situation, *that* colleague will inevitably return gratitude. Conversely, it is not shameful for a teacher to apply for help or assistance. More experienced colleagues will likely help the teacher to cope with a given problem. When a group of teachers come together, they can move mountains. Mutual assistance and support are strong weapons against teacher stress, burnout, and attrition. Mutual support makes a pedagogical staff more consolidated and collectivistic.

Share concerns and joys with the teacher working in the next-door classroom. It is necessary to notice the positive sides in the colleagues' professional activity. In building a favorable atmosphere in school, much depends on the administration, which, instead of stifling educators with bureaucratic surveillance, should help build a tightly-knit pedagogical team and render assistance when the teacher encounters a professional or personal predicament.

Enhancing the prestige of education and the teaching profession is not an easy enterprise. I am of the strong opinion that we *can* and *must* improve the situation. Schools should become shrines of knowledge, and an idyllic, pristine, and democratic pedagogical climate should permeate teacher-teacher and teacher-student relationships.

Teaching is a stressful occupation. Continual stresses may exhaust a teacher's emotional and physical state and end up with a burnout. What burnout is, what complications it can bring, and how to prevent and overcome it is the subject of the following chapter.

*Chapter 2*

# TEACHER BURNOUT

*Real love occurs only when you renounce personal benefits.*
Leo Tolstoy

*Better to give than to receive.*
Acts 20:35

Teacher burnout presents a huge dilemma for working teachers and school administrators. In fact, it is a threat to the entire systems of education. Within the previous 30 to 40 years teacher burnout has received a global attention.

## WHAT IS BURNOUT?

Burnout is known to be both a process and a result of the process. It is a gradual painful process of continual stresses, which may end with an ultimate emotional and physical exhaustion. Stress occurs when our demands exceed our resources; when it happens, the latter begins to trigger stress responses. The phenomenon of burnout includes at least three major variables (Maslach & Jackson, 1981): emotional exhaustion (a feeling of emptied emotional resources), depersonalization (when a person distances himself from others and feels that his feelings and ideas are not important), and a low sense of personal accomplishment (when an individual devalues his work).

The warning signs of the emerging burnout in teachers are a continual state of fatigue; anger and irritability in working with students; feelings of helplessness; engaging in conflicted relationships with colleagues; a negative attitude towards schooling; withdrawal from colleagues; a declining sense of professional importance; feelings of meaninglessness of the teaching activity; absence of motivation and commitment to teaching; and health problems such as hypertension (high blood pressure), insomnia, chronic bronchitis, asthma, diabetes, and intestinal disorders. A chain of stressful situations may blaze a trail to depression common signs and symptoms of which are a loss of interest in activities one enjoyed previously, feelings of worthlessness and helplessness, a desire to escape to some unknown place, easy irritability, and thoughts about committing suicide.

Studies show that Protestant teachers are significantly more depersonalized than Catholic teachers, and teachers in their 40s are more depersonalized than younger and older groups. Men are believed to have greater burnout than women. Traditionally through the years women have nurtured children and have much more interpersonal relationships with them in general (Huston, 1989). Observations also indicate that married teachers burn out less frequently than single teachers, elementary school teachers—less than middle and high school teachers, and religious teachers—less than non-religious ones.

Burnout is closely intertwined with teacher attrition and turnover. Not only after each academic year but virtually every school day tens of thousands of teachers in the world change schools or completely leave the field of education in pursuit of a better job. Some young people with teaching certificates never begin teaching, knowing beforehand about the strenuous conditions in which some working teachers find themselves.

## WHAT IS BURNOUT TRIGGERED BY?

Factors leading to stress and burnout are legion. I will enumerate a few of them.

*Sociopolitical Factors.* The general atmosphere of social and political unrest, especially when an unstable situation takes on a lingering form, inevitably makes an unfavorable impact on teachers and the whole domain of education. Sociopolitical metamorphoses may bring about a wave of incessant reorganization of the aims and strategies of teaching, various changes in the content of textbooks and other teaching materials, and an atmosphere of professional uncertainty, personal uneasiness, and suspense.

*Systematic Control.* I believe that every teacher strives to become a professional worker. The worst side of this truth is that their professionalism and expertise are constantly challenged by systematic, unexpected and, oftentimes, unfair control by school administrators, school district authorities, and ministerial officials. Unfair and unbearably frequent administrative and supervisory practices constitute a considerable blow on a teacher's emotional and physical state and self-esteem. Rigid and prejudiced supervision and accreditation of schools makes a devastating impact on the whole school life, including students. Some accreditation practices end with calamitous consequences. A school may be closed or consolidated with some other school. Some teachers and other personnel may immediately become unemployed. Other teachers may be forced to leave the school. The students may be distributed among other educational institutions. Imagine a teacher who is left jobless: Is it not an unjust and painful blow on the teacher's self-esteem? Is it not a case of an utter depersonalization of the teacher?

*Economic Factors.* As was discussed earlier, insufficient salary represents not only a major factor diminishing the status of education and the teaching profession but also a cause considerably aggravating teachers' motivation to professional activity. An unjustifiably low pay contributes to a declining sense of professional importance. Some teachers spend their own money for obtaining necessary textbooks, teaching aids, and equipment, thus further "shrinking" their already small budgets. Dissatisfaction with the salary is one of the main factors making educators leave the profession to find another job; the same factor prevents some young graduates of teacher education departments from entering the profession.

Although teachers' salaries are improved sporadically, they remain relatively low compared to the salaries of others in intellectual careers. When it comes to raising teachers' salaries, *one point* always surfaces in the minds of those who are responsible for this action: Educators appear to be the largest cohort of workers who live and work in all corners of a given country, because a teacher is needed in every place where at least a small group of families resides.

*Organizational Factors.* Poor working conditions represent a salient factor contributing to teacher stress and burnout. Across the world, teachers work in different work environments. Even in the economically developed countries their working conditions differ. If in some urban schools they may enjoy all necessary conditions for occupational safety and health, in some rural schools located just outside this urban area the work environment may be poles apart.

In the northern hemisphere, working conditions for teachers and the learning environment for students may be called relatively favorable; whereas in most of the southern countries, much should be done to improve the situation. In the countries with cold winters, teachers and learners often sit in classrooms where the temperature is much lower than the average temperature required by medical and sanitary norms. Poor air quality (specific smelly aura and a great amount of dust) is another concern. Inadequate temperatures and poor air quality are prime causes of respiratory diseases among teachers and students. The latter is a direct road to chronic diseases which, in turn, may continually cause stressful situations.

My experience shows that children are well aware of the poor conditions under which their teachers conduct lessons. When such children begin seeing better conditions and conveniences in other schools, their image of their own school and, probably, of the entire system of education starts diminishing, but their attitude to their own teachers, conversely, may change for the better. They may start regarding them with more respect for their heroic labor in unfavorable conditions.

Teachers are under the burden of "paper creation" activity. Evidence suggests that in the sphere of education paper pushing is based on "strict" hierarchical criteria, with each bureaucratic layer checking a lower layer and with the classroom teacher as the last one to endure the entire nightmare. The retired teachers unanimously acknowledge that in years long gone into history, they had not spent so much time on preparing various "documents" and discharging unnecessary duties. As for teacher educators, they experience even a greater amount of paper pushing.

*Pedagogical Factors.* One of the difficult problems plaguing teachers and students is *testing*. Strict prescriptions for testing and high requirements and accountability for its qualitative results make teachers shift much of their energy and time to the preparation and carrying out of those tests. Testing creates numerous stressful situations. Some teachers start working just for the sake of a future testing, ignoring the curriculum requirements aimed at providing learners with a good quality of knowledge and skills. This new wave of test-based teaching or, in other words, "test insanity" has become a normal practice in many educational institutions across the world.

Within the preceding decades, the high pressure and demands of testing has been severely criticized by the educational public. Educators are not against testing as a strategy of teaching and control; educators, theorists—and I myself, too—are against an inordinate pressure on testing to the detriment of other instrumental strategies of assessment.

The *low level of education* a teacher receives in college or university may be a factor engendering stressful emotional situations and eventually destroying the teacher's career. Possessing inefficient styles and manners of conducting lessons and inadequate ways of interacting with parents, low-achieving teachers, sooner or later, find themselves in a hard-nut-to-crack situation. The teaching profession becomes a burden for them.

I am inclined to seek the roots of the weak competency of young pedagogues in several causes. Some pre-service teachers do not exert sufficient efforts and time to become good specialists, but they, in general, do not reject the teaching profession. Others exert efforts but their cognitive and intellectual potential do not allow them to become high achievers (this category of graduates also plans to work in schools). Still others do not intend to work in a classroom, therefore they study only for the sake of receiving the diploma to become an "educated personality." Nevertheless, some teachers from this category, for different reasons, "eventually happen to find themselves in school classrooms."

*Personal and Psychological Factors.* Certain personality types are more prone to burnout. One such type is a perfectionist, a person who is overly dedicated to work and who constantly needs to work harder. A perfectionist always seeks to do more than he or she can possibly accomplish and tries to do better than others (Gold, 1984). Boasting extremely high expectations, perfectionists believe that anything less than ideal and perfect is unacceptable. They may constantly criticize themselves and others and, by blaming themselves and being constantly unsatisfied with their work, perfectionists may eventually damage their nervous systems.

Some teachers try to hide their stressed condition or even depression by escaping into denial. They may not confess their miserable and painful situation to their colleagues by pretending to be in a perfect state of mind. Quite intentionally, such teachers find themselves in the grip of the *syndrome of sweet lemon,* when a person turns a "sour" feeling into a "sweet" state of mind. Such an escape may diminish an emotional suffering for a short time. Ultimately, the overall state of exhaustion and attrition may "reemerge" and reestablish an even firmer grip on the individual.

*Physiological Factors.* A human being, so marvelously assembled, is prone to various ailments. With age, aches and pains more often "remind a person of their existence." Teachers are susceptible to the same physiological disorders as the representatives of other professional groups, but some diseases emerge more often in teachers than in other careers. Among teachers' professional diseases are chronic bronchitis, blood pressure, headaches, and insomnia. Educators often get colds and the flu because of frequent contacts with a great number of children, colleagues, and parents. They obtain occupational vocal disorders due to intense vocal use. Physiological problems, especially when they take on a chronic form, gradually undermine not only one's physical but also emotional state.

Our discussion of the issues of burnout thus far leads to the following important implications for school district authorities and school administrators:

## Organizing Fair Supervision

It is impossible to ban the processes of monitoring and supervision of educational institutions and educators, nor is it possible to teach students without assessing and controlling the quality of their knowledge and skills. But it is high time to *rethink the very essence of teacher supervision and evaluation.*

The educators and university faculty I often interact with unanimously agree on one important point: The supervision and evaluation of the work of the whole institution or a separate teacher should be conducted *fairly*. Instead of seeking educators' weak points or, worse, drawing all the attention on their flaws and on punitive conclusions about their work, school administrators, school district officials, and ministerial inspectors are required to render necessary assistance to schools and educators. They themselves--or with a help of some high-achieving and experienced teachers--should *practically show* some strategies of teaching and teacher-child interaction. The teaching profession needs a delicate and subtle handling. It is an occupation in which a rigid outside interference is inadmissible. Unjustifiably strict and rigorous checkups, especially when doubled with the initially planned objective to find faults or to close an educational institution, make an irretrievable strike on all school personnel, students, and on the entire enterprise of schooling.

## Creating a Favorable Working Environment

The highest degree of occupational safety and health for teachers and other school personnel should be promoted and maintained. It becomes necessary to protect educators in their place of employment from various risks such as temperatures, dilapidated school buildings that can cause harm to people, excessively long working hours, and administrative pressure. In other words, the professional activity of educators should be protected from psychological (overwork and violence), mechanical (collisions and falls from height), physical (electricity and noise), biological (virus and bacteria), and chemical (acids, noxious gases, explosion, and conflagration) hazards ("Occupational safety," 2011).

As for educators, I give them two pieces of good advice:

## Complement Your Colleagues' Work

Teachers need to be complemented for their jobs, especially if a job is well done. In fact, everyone honestly earning bread is worth praise. If your compliments are sincerely delivered, compliments pay off. A sincere compliment will reduce the weight of a stress or emotional tension and instill a motivating impulse in a teacher's work. Taking into consideration Dale Carnegie's recommendations on how to handle people and my own observations, I offer a few suggestions for teachers:

- Take a sincere interest in the work of your colleagues.
- Listen attentively to your colleagues, especially when they experience a stressful situation and need a help.
- Encourage them to reveal the whole picture of their predicaments.
- Try to understand and consider the pluses and minuses of the teaching process from your colleague's viewpoint.
- Avoid criticizing and condemning your co-workers.
- Support and share the values they value and share.
- Call attention to your colleagues' and administrator's mistakes and reproaches indirectly.
- Instill a feeling of significance in the people you work with.

## Maintain Favorable Relations with the Loved Ones

Maintaining an appropriate climate and relationships in the family is a key determinant adding to the teacher's successful professional activity in school. Family is a prime cell of society. The teacher spends most time in the circle of the spouse, children, and, probably, father and mother and relatives.

Family quarrels, strained relationships with the spouse, misunderstandings between the teacher and his own children and other disagreements immediately impact the professional work of the teacher. One trivial discord with the spouse in the morning may linger in the mind of the teacher all day. It means that the teacher's emotional state may be spoiled for the whole day and probably for days to come. So will the ways of conducting lessons and interacting with children and colleagues. There were a number of similar occasions in my own professional practice as teacher educator, when I, after coming to class with a burden of a recent problem in my family, was in a stressful mood in working with pre-service teachers

In passing, an episode from the past has emerged in my memory.

Once I attended a public lecture delivered by a psychologist on the impact of family life on the quality of one's professional activity and success. The lecturer provided us with interesting insights on how to keep favorable relationships with family members, close relatives, and with neighbors. She told us how a stress in the family can worsen an emotional state of a person when he steps on his working place. In the end, she posed a question, "My dear friends and colleagues! After talking about these vital topics, I would like to ask, quite of a sudden, a somewhat odd question: 'Who is a completely happy married person?'"

The listeners began giving their answers. Lastly, she complimented the people on their interesting considerations and said, "Thank you for participating in the discussion. As for me, I assume that a fully happy married person is the one who, in a cheerful mood, hurries to work in the morning because the person loves his occupation, and after the working day is over, he rushes to his family because he cherishes his loved ones. This person is the happiest married individual on earth."

After the lecture I was driving home digesting what the psychologist had inspired us with. I asked myself if I was a happy individual after all. It appeared that I was only partly happy according to the lecturer's theory, because sometimes I did not go to my office in happy spirits and sometimes, after working hours, I was reluctant to return to my family.

When one is in a prolonged state of emotional breakdown or feels an approaching depression, it is better to focus attention off the condition that nags a person. I recommend a teacher to find an interesting theme for conversation with some other people (colleagues, spouse, children, or neighbors); visit a place that renews; participate in sports; do physical exercises; view a good movie or listen to mild, soothing music; or read some religious material. Reading a good book on how to combat stress and a depressive state will inevitably help.

One of the pervasive causes of teacher burnout is the inability to manage the class, which will be the focus of our attention in the proceeding section.

*Chapter 3*

# CLASSROOM MANAGEMENT METAMORPHOSES

*Small children give you a headache, big children a heartache.*
Russian proverb

*In the right environment normality comes naturally, by itself.*
Maria Montessori

Evidence suggests that classroom management, an important aspect of teachers' professional activity, dominates educators' concerns from student teaching till the end of their careers. Not only in teaching but also in other aspects of life much depends on how we organize, control, and provide a necessary environment for the favorable functioning of an activity. The activity of maintaining an effective family is one such example. Without a proper management of all the familial enterprises and without a mutual understanding, there may hardly unfold favorable relationships between the spouses and between parents and children. Similar is the case with classroom management. When things do not go well with classroom discipline and when the teacher is unable to organize proper instruction, there may occur serious problems in his or her work.

Classroom control and teaching are closely linked and intertwined. The higher the degree of teachers' professional competency, the more motivated and occupied are students, and fewer cases may arise with discipline, and fewer students sit idle in class. Conversely, the more able teachers are in coping with discipline, the easier is the process of teaching and learning. However, an effective classroom management does not *always* guarantee a proper academic atmosphere, and a highly effective instruction can not *always* reduce *all* behavior disruption problems to the minimum.

## INABILITY TO CURB DISCIPLINE

Classroom organization and management are not the equal of discipline. Classroom management includes all possible initiatives teachers undertake to create a productive working environment for children to achieve in class and after-class activities. In fact, the effects of proper classroom management are often felt outside the school boundaries and "reach" the places where children gain and digest knowledge and information after classes--libraries, computer centers, and home environments. Discipline is narrower in meaning and scope and deals with children's behavior while they are involved in cognitive activity and with how teachers can cope with this behavior.

The commonest conduct problems among secondary school students are the following: disrupting the teacher's speech; refusing to speak with the teacher; sleeping and lying idle on the table; teasing peers; engaging in quarrels with peers; whistling and inexplicable singing; threatening peers physically and verbally; using mobile phones; walking about and leaving the classroom; throwing objects; flirting and other inappropriate sexual behavior; and getting involved in physical fights.

In the 1960s-1980s, Western educators visiting secondary and higher educational institutions in the former Soviet Union used to criticize the strict discipline reigning in classrooms and auditoria and compare it to the Western standards of classroom management, which they had considered to be really democratic. The authors of numerous journal and newspaper articles condemned the Soviet style of classroom management and control. At the same time, Western scholars and educators had been urging young home-grown teachers to start with a strict discipline in class and persuading educators that the inability to control children was a major cause of teacher burnout and teacher attrition. In their criticism, they were quite right! But I have always been wondering at such a paradoxical situation.

After vigorously knocking at Russia's borders, democracy is now taking root on its soil. "Having played with democracy in the classroom" for a while, Russian educators gradually came to the conclusion that democratic styles of classroom control do not help in all situations and that it is unwise to forget old and reliable styles of managing the class.

# CLASS SIZE

An acute problem gaining notice in the countries of South America, Africa, and Asia is population growth. On these continents, an overcrowded class is a natural phenomenon. Large-size classes are expected to produce decreased academic achievement, ill-behaved students, and a less individualized instruction. Teachers are more stressed in large classes and schools than in smaller ones. I have never in my life met an educator who was in favor of large-size classes.

In some countries, this demographic upsurge entails an increase in class size; in other nation states, a demographic decrease, conversely, leads to a decrease in class and school size, which may lead to various reorganizations of educational institutions. For instance, Russia's overall population was steadily decreasing in the 1990s-2010s. As a result, a considerable number of small town and rural schools became tiny educational institutions with miniature classes. Some of these schools were combined so as to form larger schools; others were completely closed with all the negative consequences for educators and students and for the future survival of local communities.

# GETTING LOST IN THE VORTEX OF DIVERSITY

Many teachers experience difficulty working with a diversity of students and get stressed and frustrated easily, because they have to cope with various behavioral patterns that children from different ethnic and cultural groups bring to school. Human diversity is a phenomenon encompassing a whole range of racial, ethnic, linguistic, religious, social class, and gender issues intertwined in contemporary countries. For instance, ethnic diversity is represented by a multitude of peoples inhabiting the earth; religious diversity, by the world religions such as Christianity, Islam, Judaism, Buddhism and other religions and denominations; socioeconomic diversity, by people belonging to different socioeconomic levels; and urban/rural diversity, by a plethora of lifestyles of people inhabiting urban and rural settings. On a smaller scale, human diversity embraces value systems, attitudes, age, customs and traditions, cuisines, styles of clothing and many other explicit and implicit aspects of human behavior and existence.

Continually increasing and changing, diversity makes a huge impart on educational practices by challenging educators with new dilemmas as well as with old quandaries shrouded with novel concerns. Educators have to deal with students from different cultural and ethnic background and implement strategies to address the cognitive and cultural needs of each learner.

Following are several strategies teachers may find helpful in monitoring students:

## Begin with a Firm Discipline

Set up proper classroom organization and control from the very beginning of a successive school year. Some teachers start developing plans of action to regain control only after experiencing a series of behavioral incidents or when they have completely lost control of the class. If disruptive behaviors become a norm, it will be next to impossible to curb the guilty children. If you start with a serious monitoring of discipline, you can always relax some of your regulations when the circumstances permit. Certain problems in classroom management may be manifestations of larger causes. In such circumstances, an effective classroom order is largely dependent on unified efforts of educators, parents, and students.

It is necessary to announce certain rules right from the start. For instance, you may strongly request that during lessons children should not chew gums, talk loudly, walk about the class without permission of the teacher, bring unnecessary things, come to school in indecent and sexually provocative attire, and should not engage in quarrels and fights. In some European countries I saw similar rules written on a sheet of paper and pinned near the board or on other visible places.

When enforcing disciplinary actions or rules, be consistent and fair. Such rules are designed not for punishing a pupil any time he or she breaks a precept but for establishing a better order. Be tolerant and remind pupils of a rule as many times as possible. Only when a pupil starts breaking or disrupting the overall climate at the lesson continually and nothing helps, you can report the case to the administrator and parents.

In maintaining classroom order, teachers often have to deal with egocentric students who create problems by trying to draw attention of their peers and teachers to themselves. Especially egocentric are adolescents. According to David Elkind (cited in Santrock, 2002), egocentrism can be dissected into two types of social thinking—imaginary audience and personal fable. Imaginary audience involves students' belief that other people are as interested in them as they themselves are. It also involves attention-getting behavior triggered by the desire to be noticed and to be "on stage." The phenomenon of personal fable involves a student's sense of uniqueness and invincibility. Egocentrically minded students want to be at the center of attention. They feel that they are the "important people," the actors; whereas the class and the teacher are the audience. By drawing attention to themselves by all possible means, they often create uniquely problematic situations.

At the same time I caution educators against using extreme strategies and approaches exceeding the boundaries dictated by reason and by physical human capacities. Let the kids be busy but avoid excessive academic pressure on them. *Do not always equate their abilities with yours.*

## Involve All Students in Cognitive Activity

Children often become inattentive and seek some other activity other than academic because they have no distinct assignments. They do not know what to do and how to do. All children should be fully occupied from the beginning to the end of each lesson. Attentively monitoring pupils, you have to notice all the children who have finished doing their successive assignments and immediately provide them with new tasks. If you see more than one idle student, you can organize work in pairs or a small-group activity.

## Monitor Students' Work

Involving all students in working is one thing. Another thing is that you should continuously monitor and guide their creative and cognitive activity. The entire class should be in your field of vision. Experienced teachers see the whole class and what each student is doing just by one quick glance somewhere at the middle of the whole cluster of kids. Have all the students started working? Have they all opened their textbooks and copybooks? Have they all performed the required assignment on computer screen? Are there any distracted students in class? Have all learners understood the essence of the recommended task? These and many other similar questions should always be on your mind. While students are busy working, you may walk around the room checking their activity and progress. When you are in close proximity to students, they are likely to cherish your personal attention and to be motivated to further cognitive activity.

## Avoid Free Time

When planning a lesson, always try to prepare some additional material if the lesson runs short. When you finish a lesson with several minutes left until the official end of it, students may immediately raise havoc by talking loudly and putting their stuff into their bags. At such moments, teachers usually get frustrated because it becomes difficult for them to regain order.

I myself always have at hand some additional assignments or tests for my students during seminars. Not often but sometimes my lectures run short. When it occurs, I pose a series of questions to make sure they have understood the target theme or tell them some additional material on the target topic.

## Familiarize Students with Yourself

Give students your email address and announce your boundaries for communication. Once in a while present a visual depiction of your life by showing them some photos from your school and college life. Share insights with them about some memorable episodes from your life and professional experience. You may show them the pictures of your pet if you own one. Involve them into photo and video sessions, take pictures and video fragments of the class.

Tell them what you like and dislike as a teacher. When I began working as an English language teacher, I told my eighth- and ninth-grade students, right in the beginning of the academic year, that I like when students do not bother each other during the lesson, when they raise hands and actively participate in class activities, write down all the unknown English words in the vocabulary, read a foreign text several times aloud at home, and retell it afterwards by their own words. Believe me or not, but this strategy worked relatively well!

## Get to Know Every Child Well

I strongly recommend teachers to allocate time and get to know children's genealogical trees, including parents, sisters, brothers, grandparents, and relatives. Children's physical features and characteristics such as face, eyes, hair color, the body configuration, manners of gesticulation, and voice tend to resemble those of parents and, to some extent, of other ancestors on the genealogical line. Likewise, a wide range of behavioral and socioemotional characteristics and traits are also inherited.

When a child inherits positive traits, so much the better. Quite often, a child falls a victim of negative genealogical inheritance. An episode from my personal conversation with Oleg Semenov, a teacher from Moscow, is vivid on my mind.

Once, one of Oleg's students, a sixth-grade girl, told him downright, "If you do not put me a good grade, I will do something with myself, and the blame will fall on you."

Oleg put the girl a grade she deserved, and she seemed to have got offended with the teacher, but time gradually healed the case. Next time, the same student, without any reason, told Oleg that she would throw herself from the window sill if he did not stop making remarks on her behavior. (She had been very talkative and had kept distracting her peers from academic activity). Several other times, having got offended with the teacher for some trivial reasons, she left the classroom slamming the door behind her. Other teachers, Oleg's colleagues, had also complained about her. The causes of their complaints had been similar: She had threatened educators that she would destroy herself if they did not fulfill her "requests."

Oleg Semenov disembarked on a pedagogical investigation of the girl's genealogical line. He made a closer acquaintance with her parents and some of the relatives. In the long run, he came to learn that her father, in a drunken state, had wanted to destroy himself several times, but each time people nearby had saved him. Her father's sister had also wanted to commit a suicide by cutting her veins on a hand. Luckily, she had survived. Another relative of hers, a young man, had hung himself and left his wife and a baby.

Worried and anxious, Oleg consulted licensed specialists about the girl's behavior. They attributed her disruptive conduct and attempts to commit suicide to the syndrome of self-destruction that she could have inherited from her father and/or other relatives. To be on the safe side, Oleg gave a notice in writing to the medical center.

It is also imperative to keep in mind that both environmental and hereditary factors, or nurture and nature, make an influence on child development. Not all ancestral traits are inherited by a child. Equally, not all socioemotional and behavioral predispositions may be a result of genealogical inheritance.

## Avoid Discussing a Student's Misbehavior Publicly

It is advisable that you get some small problems back on track in the classroom by nodding the head, movements of your hand, or by short phrases. Criticizing misbehaving learners in front of others tend to injure the pride of the "law-breakers." A disturber of classroom climate may find himself in a frustrated state. If "open punishment" of a misbehaving student becomes a norm, the student may lose interest in learning at all. When a pupil is constantly punished, his classmates may also ridicule or even try to avoid him.

I recommend dealing with disciplinary problems privately, face-to-face. How long should the teacher tolerate a misbehaving child? The teacher is required to tolerate and work with the child until he stops to disrupt the working atmosphere and changes for the better. Obviously, if the teacher alone is unable to handle the problem, the administrator and parents should be involved to put things right.

## Deal with Praise and Punishment Correctly

Throughout human history, avoiding these two phenomena has been virtually impossible in child rearing practices. Both have advantages and disadvantages. In its many forms, praise provides students with a hope that their behavior and manners are decent. Praise helps raise their motivation to be good learners and diligent students. Praise works wonders. Praise may lose its pedagogical power if a particular student is complimented much and often. This student may start awaiting praise for any minor "positive action." It may so happen that this student will begin behaving and working only for the sake of an expression of approval and admiration from educators and other adults.

Punishment can stop an undesirable behavior and help students to discriminate an acceptable from unacceptable behavior. Punishment can lead to aggression and negatively influence a student's self-concept. A child can also get used to being punished and start disregarding the teacher's punitive actions. The child may come to the conclusion, "Well, I am in bad repute with the teacher and students, and nothing will help whether I behave or not."

## Consider Students' Learning Styles

As we know, children bring to school a variety of learning preferences and styles of interpersonal interaction, especially in culturally pluralistic settings. Students' learning styles may be determined by sociopolitical, religious, cultural, academic, technological, environmental, and physical factors. In fact, every student possesses some learning preference. One student possesses only one way of learning; another may use multiple cognitive preferences. Still another one can easily adapt to any new circumstances and ways of teaching. Concentrating on students' learning preferences is one side of the problem. The other side is selecting an appropriate instructional style that may match a particular manner of learning. (Sinagatullin, 2009b).

In practice, mismatches often occur between students' learning styles and the teacher's instructional styles, which sometimes leads to psychologically unfavorable consequences. When such cases occur, students tend to become inattentive, begin to receive low grades, and often get discouraged about the subject, the teacher, and the school and its overall academic atmosphere. Such course of events also makes a negative impact on the teacher, who may start "recouping his losses" by becoming captious and unjust toward students or start questioning his own professional competence. (p. 97)

One of the best ways of correlating teaching style and learning style is following the law of equilibrium, i.e. creating an optimal teaching/learning environment. I recommend educators:

- not to change culture-related traditions of learning and behavior by forcefully introducing new strategies of instruction and interaction with children. In any case, innovative strategies will gradually push their way through;
- to use a balance of instructional strategies. Approach children partly in the manner they prefer and partly in a less preferred style (Felder & Henriques, 1995);
- to keep in mind children's cultural, genealogical, and socioemotional characteristics in teaching and building a favorable classroom climate.

To manage and control teaching and learning is not so easy as one might imagine. You can not handle it by saying, "Sesame door, open!" This gargantuan door *may* open to the teacher, but much effort, tolerance, and expertise are needed. Equally, the teacher cannot say, "Well, I will first devote three minutes to establishing a good order, then, will start explaining the new material." Classroom management is a part of teaching and not something standing separately, something that precedes or proceeds instruction. The class is being managed in the process of teaching. Managing students' work should be embedded in all cells of teaching. Classroom management is an eternal process occurring simultaneously with teaching, checking homework, writing tests, organizing group work, singing songs, reciting poems, and with surfing the Internet. It is a normal, day-to-day work with the whole class and individually with each learner. The ideal form of classroom management will occur only when the teacher conducts a lesson "without knowing" what classroom management is. In other words, when the teacher lives a life of educating children.

Becoming an effective classroom organizer and manager requires concentration, hard work, tolerance, and time. No one theory and instructional method is applicable to all cultures or to one ethnic group on all occasions. Insightful educators choose a technique compatible with a given diverse group of students or with a single learner, and they skillfully mold their strategies to address the needs of their disciples.

Quite a lot of elementary, middle, and high schools are located in rural settings and called *rural schools*. Like their urban counterparts, they also require that teachers use effective classroom management strategies. At the same time, rural educational institutions have their own specificity. Why should state and governmental officials draw paramount attention to rural education and, on the whole, to rural life? Why do rural schools experience hard times? Why do young educators refuse to seek a job in a rural or small town setting and, instead, seek a better life in a metro area? Step by step, I will try to briefly investigate these and related enigmas in the next chapter.

# Chapter 4

# RURAL EDUCATION:
# A FORGOTTEN LEGACY?

*I roamed the countryside searching for answers to things*
*I did not understand.*
Leonardo da Vinci

*Ironically, rural America has become viewed by a growing*
*number of Americans as having a high quality of life*
*not because of what it has, but rather because of what it does not have.*
Don A. Dillman

I believe that we, human beings, are one monolithic race; nevertheless, urban and rural residents' lifestyles and their attitudes to educating the young have always differed to a greater and lesser extent. In some countries of Asia, Latin America, and Africa, these differences may be distinct and pervasive, whereas in some European countries such differences are not so noticeable. One such country is the Netherlands, where there is almost no difference between urban and rural settings or between urban and rural education. Dutch villages are picturesque and economically wealthy.

When I first visited this country, I was taken to a hotel from the airport by car. As we were driving through a well-planned and beautiful settlement, I asked my Dutch colleague at the wheel, "Will you be so kind as to show me some day a village in this country?"

Amazed, he looked up at me, "What you are seeing around is a typical village. We are now driving through it."

I looked around and, seeing beautifully painted houses and paved streets, formulated another question: "If this is a village, then, is there some festive event or fair going on in this settlement today? They have embellished and decorated the houses so exquisitely!"

"They are always in such order and look so magnificently," said my colleague and smiled.

The ratio of urban to rural populations differs across the world. For example, in 2010, in Monaco the ratio of urban to rural population was 100% and 0%; in Belgium, 97.4 and 2.6; in the United States, 82 and 18; in the United Kingdom, 79.5 and 20.5; in Russia, 73.1 and 26.9; in China, 46.1 and 53.9; in Congo, 34.6 and 65.4; and in the Solomon Islands, 18.2 and 81.8 (Janssen, 2011).

# RURAL EDUCATION

Rural education has traditionally played a significant role in ameliorating people's living standards, advancing the agricultural sector of economy, and in resolving the fate of the land. Not without reason Theodore Roosevelt said that the "men and women on the farms stand for what is fundamentally best and most needed in our American life" (cited in Fuller, 1982, p. 219).

Meanwhile, a range of issues directly related to rural education and rural teacher education have been set aside or ignored as questions of minor importance or even *forgotten* all together. It seems that people in higher echelons of power are unaware of the existence of some vital problems facing rural schools, rural teachers, and rural students. For instance, in the United States, rural education lags behind urban levels and rural schools experience financial constraints and shortages of trained teachers. In China, rural schools lack teachers and only about 15% of rural children enter high school. In India, rural schools experience a shortage of well qualified teachers and lack necessary technology and teaching aids. There is also a chronic shortage of teachers in Nigerian rural schools ("Summer Volunteer," 2007; "Review of rural education," 2011; "Greatest needs," 2011). As for standardized achievement tests, rural students usually score worse than their urban counterparts.

## PROBLEMS OF RURAL SCHOOLS

There is a range of problems rural schools face. Let us take a look at some of them.

*Teacher Shortages.* Lack of teachers makes a considerable number of rural educators teach in a variety of subject areas, some outside their field of competence. Some young graduates become discouraged with the working conditions and salaries and leave rural schools to find a better job in an urban setting.

*Financial Difficulties.* Rural schools need twice as much financial support. Because of financial constraints, most rural schools can not afford modern technology, necessary teaching aids, or essential didactic literature. Often, the total amount of money allocated for a school depends on a number of students studying in that school. Unlucky are smaller rural institutions. It is lack of money that compels most schools to build their own diminutive budgets.

*Sociogeographic Difficulties.* In schools located in isolated and remote areas, children have to cover long distances to get to school and back home. Busing is not always organized properly in rural settings, and the roads are not always in good maintenance. Climatic difficulties increase the problem of transportation. In cold or, conversely, hot climatic zones, children have to overcome even harsher conditions as they pass long ways through forests, mountains, or deserts. In winter the roads may be snow-covered. After rainfalls they may be extremely muddy or slippery. In remote, isolated, and poverty-stricken regions, students, teachers, and all residents in general often experience little or no access to modern technology, healthcare institutions, sports grounds, theaters, museums, exhibitions and other socioeconomic and cultural assets.

*School Closure and Consolidation.* Each year hundreds of rural schools in both northern and southern hemispheres are closed or consolidated. Despite the protests from local communities, official structures may "discharge their obligations as planned." To settle the future of a certain school, in some countries governments set criteria whether a school should be closed or combined with some neighboring institution. The closure of the school in a village tells not only on teachers' professional careers and their lives but also on the whole rural infrastructure. For example, in Russia the populations of a considerable number of rural communities have declined lately. Thus, the loss of a rural school in a village leads to the demise of the village itself. In this respect I recall Ermolaev's wise statement (1991):

The fate and future of the land that feeds us all, the fate of peasantry, villages and the rate and quality of social development depend on our long-suffering rural schools; lastly, if we close this sequence of interconnected chain, the prosperity, or, on the contrary, the poverty and backwardness of our nation also depend on rural schools. (p. 14)

Migratory processes further worsen the situation in rural areas and with rural schools. Young rural residents tend to move to urban regions in search of a better life. As a result, rural schools enroll fewer children. Schools with diminishing enrollments may sooner or later be doomed to closure, consolidation or other reconstructions. Young urban residents and college graduates do not dare to come to villages, preferring a good job in metropolitan areas.

*Engaging in Physical Activity.* Rural girls and boys have to spend more time involved in agricultural and household work. These occupations require extra time and effort. Children and especially adolescents help their parents in growing vegetables and fruit and in raising cattle and poultry. Engaged in such activities after classes and on weekends, rural adolescents lack sufficient time to study at home. In discussing the issues of physical labor, I do not suggest any hint of forced or bonded labor, when parents or other adults make little ones work in the fields, farms, or as wage laborers. These and other inhumane practices are prohibited by corresponding international laws.

*The Inferiority Complex.* Some rural students feel uneasy and constrained about being a rural dweller and living far from a refined world. They tend to consider themselves as worth nothing but a "villager" and "dung scraper." They may strongly internalize this psychological syndrome of inferiority. Being aware of their low social status, some rural students steadily lose their desire to continue living in the rural setting. Upon graduation, or even earlier, they are likely to leave village for an urban settlement to get "urbanized" or become a city resident. In this case, too, the migration of young boys and girls to metropolises has an unfavorable effect on rural school, rural education, and rural socioeconomic infrastructure.

*Teaching in Multi-Grade Classrooms.* In tiny rural elementary and secondary schools, some educators have to teach in multi-grade classrooms. I interacted with a great number of teacher educators and graduate students in many countries of the world. I used to ask my typical question that sounded approximately like this, "Will you be able to work in a multi-grade classroom at a rural school?" The majority of graduates I talked with had no notion of what multi-grading is. Others had only some vague idea about this phenomenon. Only one young teacher, Hana Homolova, in Prague, Czech Republic, articulately described me the essence of multi-grading.

What does multi-grading mean? In multi-grade classes pupils are gathered from different grades and, consequently, different age levels into one class. Educators teach several programs to the children of this unified grade, i.e. they teach more than one discipline and grade simultaneously. Why do schools have to build such classes? Because they are unable to hire separate teachers for each grade level in elementary classes and for each discipline in middle and senior classes when such grades encompass a small number of students each. Mixed-age classes keep a teacher extremely busy and strained because the teacher has to switch from the requirements of one curriculum to those of another keeping in mind and tracking the programs of several grades.

*Psychological Uncertainty.* Like in urban areas, teachers in rural schools encounter similar stressful situations; but I want to mention a uniquely rural syndrome many rural teachers complain about: the feeling of psychological uncertainty. The school a teacher works in may be closed or combined with some other school. As a result, the teacher may become unemployed. The fate of the village the school is situated in may also be precarious and uncertain. Some young teachers who choose to teach in rural schools experience difficulty solving personal problems such as, for example, meeting a reliable partner and getting married. It is this very conundrum that deters most young educators from seeking a job in a rural setting.

Once, at the Graduation Ceremony held annually at Birsk State Socio-Pedagogical Academy, I engaged in a conversation with Zina Karpova, a young diploma holder or, as Russians say, a "newly-baked specialist." In the process of our chat I came to learn that Zina had been born and raised in a remote village; therefore I asked her if she wanted to return to her village to teach in her beloved school.

"Never," she said abruptly, "even though I love my school and often remember my teachers who had provided me with ample knowledge and manners."

As if interrupting her chain of thoughts, I said, "By the way, …they are going to raise rural teachers' salaries in the nearest future."

Zina hesitated a little. "M-m-m… Working as a teacher is one thing. Yes, I will be earning my living. I will be educating little ones, thus making contribution to my motherland. But I will unlikely settle my personal matters, like building a family and raising children. My home village and the villages surrounding it have become tiny settlements owing to the exodus of young people and young families to metro areas

in search of a better job and a better life. Almost all people in these
villages are now retired, and the average age of the youngest male
residents is over 60 ...."
    I understood quickly what Zina's implicit hint meant.

As there is more parental contact in rural settings, some educators I used
to interact with complain about dealing with parents as a source of stress;
others, conversely, regard close and frequent contacts with families as a factor
variably influencing their professional activity.

Scholars, researchers, and policy makers often lack the knowledge and full
information they need to design constructive policies to address rural issues.
To address the needs of rural education and rural schools, local and
governmental policy-makers should:

- encourage world-wide initiatives to address the basic sociocultural
  and educational needs of rural youth;
- place the issues of rural education at the center of attention of the
  ministries responsible for education, finances, agriculture, and health.
  They should cooperate and seek constructive ways to ameliorate rural
  education, raise the status and prestige of rural schools in the overall
  agricultural infrastructure, and enhance the living standards and
  working conditions of rural and small town residents. It is necessary
  to sustain all small and tiny rural schools because small-size classes
  and schools positively influence academic achievement and promote
  better classroom management;
- create and endorse policies facilitating the recruitment and retention
  of not only rural teachers but also qualified administrators. A school
  principal is virtually responsible for everything, beginning with a nail
  driven on a wall to the IQ test results of every school graduate.

Pre-service teachers who were born in a rural setting and 'breathed" a
rural life do not normally shun a rural reality. It is easier to recruit them to
country schools upon graduation. Harder is the case with metrocentric
graduates who are less likely to choose employment in rural educational
institutions.

In general, most rural teachers tend to diligently discharge their
obligations, despite continually arising difficulties. In addition, I offer the
following recommendations to a rural teacher:

## Foster Cooperative Learning Strategies

Rural children, teenagers, and adults tend to be high-context people. All school children know almost everything about everybody in the school premises and local community. They also tend to be collectivistically minded. In these circumstances it is preferable for you to use cooperative approaches, which foster mutual responsibility and develop in students a compassionate and tolerant attitude to each other. As classes are typically small, group discussion is also an effective method of learning. In group work, pupils are aware of their responsibility for the success of the whole group. In other cases, use an appropriate instructional style that best suits the cognitive preference of a given student or suits a given situation.

## Cope with Multigrade Strategies

Fundamentally, teaching and child development pursues similar objectives in all societies: We prepare the young for work, life, and for making the world a better place. Nevertheless, organizing a teaching/learning process in multigrade classrooms is a unique and biggest challenge for rural teachers. Multigrading is not a new method of grouping learners. It is probably as old as humankind. Providing one believes in Darwin's theory of evolution, then it is easy to imagine how ancient tribesmen, when instructing and admonishing their youngsters, used to gather them into one group that could represent nothing but a multi-age cluster of children.

Following are several instructional dimensions for multigrade teachers:

- Promote flexible organizational strategies within and across grade levels assembled in one class. All learners of all grade levels should be engaged in work during the lesson. After working with one grade level (group), you may provide this grade with another task and quickly switch to working with another, "older" or "younger" grade level.
- Effectively use time. Not a single minute should pass idle, except for the time required, perhaps, for a short break for doing some physical or other relaxation exercises.
- Prepare and use extra assignments in store for all grade levels if some finish their tasks before others.

- Promote cooperative methods of teaching and learning. Cooperation is a necessity in multigrading. Share instructional responsibilities with older students while working with younger ones. Also engage same-age students in cooperation.
- Foster students' responsibility for their own learning. Whatever strategy the teacher uses, learning is ultimately an individual and independent process for each one child. Helping others, each student should help himself or herself. Foster student-centered approaches wherever possible. Evidence indicates that multigrading does not negatively affect academic achievement and child development. At the same time, multigrade instruction requires maximum energy and effective organizational and instructional skills.

## Use Folk Pedagogy

A rural school, especially if located in a multicultural setting, sets a favorable stage for utilizing folk pedagogical practices. These are those which are traditionally used by parents, relatives, and community members and which may have been passed over by their predecessors. Throughout recorded history, folk pedagogy has played a crucial role in child development (Volkov, 1999; Akhiyarov, 2000; Sinagatullin, 2002). The goals and means of folk pedagogy of different cultural and ethnic groups have much in common because folk pedagogy promotes values such as tolerance, honesty, respect for parents and old people, health, and industriousness. Folk pedagogy is interrelated with multicultural education, which uses the means and outcomes of folk pedagogy research to address the diversity of students.

There is a variety of means of folk pedagogy among different peoples. Frequently used in many cultures are play, folk music, folk dances, fairy tales, and proverbs and sayings. Factors determining children's cognitive, intellectual, and physical development are the natural environment, family, religion, and holidays and festive events. For example, play is a natural activity in preparing children for adulthood and social life and is often linked to other activities such as riddles, fairy-tales, and dances. Vygotsky (1991) maintains that play is inherent not only in human beings but also in animals, therefore this fact contains some biological meaning; otherwise play could not have existed. "Play is the first school of thought for a child" (p. 127).

In rural areas child development is largely influenced by natural environment. In the indigenous pedagogical traditions of Native Americans, the categories of man and nature are closely interconnected. The unity of these entities is looked at as one of the harmonies of life. Likewise, in Russia, in the folk traditions of Bashkirs, Tatars, Mari, Chuvashes, Chukchi, and Evenks, the categories of man and nature are intertwined entities.

## Love Rural Children and Rural People

Normally rural children are more diligent and industrious than their urban counterparts. They tend to possess higher moral and personal characteristics, are less pretentious, more obedient and field-dependent. As rural kids are closer to the land and nature, they are physically stronger. They are not as ambitious as their urban peers in satisfying their consumer interest.

Rural residents tend to be patriots of their land and their occupations, which are often passed from generation to generation. They try to sustain native customs and cultural traditions. Most important, *rural residents value and respect the teacher and the teaching profession.* Is it possible not to admire and not to love rural children and their parents?

## Cherish Rural Land and Country Life

Even though you may not have been born in the countryside, nevertheless, it is *your* land because all people in your nation state and in the world taken together are fundamentally one flock. You are an individual who is not only bound to educate rural children but also assigned to keep the school and local community united. It may so happen that you choose to return to the land you had been born in and your ancestors had lived in, and if you take roots in this land, you will be the happiest person who has ever lived under the sun!

## Benefit from Living in a Rural Setting

Living in a rural setting has its advantages over residing in an urban area. To an urban dweller or an incidental observer, a rural setting may seem less pleasing to the eye. In reality, most rural settings are not spoiled and devastated by human intrusion and characterized by a naturally idyllic and bucolic atmosphere, an aura of peacefulness, and by separation from a turbulent city life, a life amidst triangles and quadrangles and a life of rushing automobiles. Rural residents are likely to breathe a fresher air, drink purer water, and consume organic vegetables and fruits. They may easily replace their cars with bicycles and "become cowboys" if they venture to ride on horseback.

A rural setting or countryside is the perfect choice for your family picnic, fishing, jogging, intimate getaways or other weekend and vacation retreats. In rural locales teachers can easier and probably cheaper solve some problems of the organization of their living conditions—building a house, raising cattle and poultry, and growing vegetables and fruit—in close collaboration with local authorities and local communities. People working the land can always lend a helping hand to a teacher in unyielding circumstances.

## Have a Positive Attitude to Working and Living in a Rural Setting

Most rural teachers are doing a great job for enhancing rural education and refining and strengthening rural communities. If you are a rural teacher, be sure that you are adorning and beautifying the rural setting you are working in! You might not have thought of it yet: You are an educated person upon whom many villagers are dependent on! Fill your heart with pride that you belong to a prestigious profession. As for difficulties, they are plenty in all occupations. Have a positive attitude about being a rural educator.

## Continually Enhance Your Professional and Global Competency

You should know that rural teachers' professional and global competency must even surpass that of urban teachers. A considerable number of rural residents and their children throughout the world live in poor conditions and, even today, many rural children are deprived of access to the Internet and other means of mass media. They spend their school years in remote and impoverished settings without seeing and enjoying much of sociocultural assets that are plentiful in urban areas. A rural teacher is often the only source of information about the world surrounding rural pupils.

Ameliorating rural education requires *resources, persistence, tolerance,* and *understanding* on the part of all existing hierarchical levels. When monitored by wise and clever minds, these four totalities, taken together, will work wonders! I will say more to what has been discussed: Rural schools are *lifeblood* of rural communities. In a sense, we all or almost all have rural roots.

Rural teachers work in specific living conditions: in villages with few modern conveniences and services and in remote and isolated places. They make their pedagogical contribution in the coldest areas of Canada and Russia; the arid regions of the Sahara Desert; the jungles of South America, Africa, and Asia; the mountainous locales of the Himalayas, the Andes, and the Alps; the sparsely populated areas of Russia; and in the island enclaves of the Pacific Ocean. They must deserve the greatest praise and recognition!

If a local school lives and prospers, so will the local community. Children will grow physically robust and morally pure. The local community will progress, crops will grow, cattle will graze on the fields and mountain slopes, and fishermen will enjoy good catches. Improving rural education must be a sacred commitment and cause of human civilization!

Do rural teachers live in seclusion? Due to objective circumstances, some do. But not only rural teachers but also most of their urban counterparts, for different reasons, seldom venture to participate in teachers' conferences and seminars, see interesting places in their own countries and abroad, and seldom share insights with their counterparts from other ethnic and cultural groups. Discussing these and other related points is the goal of the next chapter.

*Chapter 5*

# LIVING IN SECLUSION

*A day of traveling will bring a basketful of learning.*
Vietnamese proverb

*It is better to bask on the beaches of Hurghada*
*than to look attentively at the Great Pyramid.*
Erich von Däniken

Since the start of my pedagogical career I have met hundreds of educators in Russia and other countries who lead a secluded life. They spend their free time and vacations far from the "turbulent civilization:" in the family circle; building a house; working in their gardens; helping their children to become independent; taking care of their parents, children or grandchildren; fishing; roaming in the wilderness or camping near the water; or moonlighting. Most of them are compelled to live, work, and stay in their residential areas for years, even during vacations, without traveling and seeing the world.

## SEEING THE WORLD

One aspect clearly and uniquely distinguishing the teaching profession from other occupations is that a *teacher is obliged to know everything*. In a sense, a teacher has to be a walking encyclopedia. Is it possible for a human being to know everything? Obviously, not! But it is absolutely possible to constantly strive to *learn and see as much as possible!* What is important is that the teacher should have a motivation to be on the way to fulfilling this sacred task.

Educators and students can surf the Internet and "visit" any place on earth, download the required information, and bring it to the classroom. In other cases they may direct students to numerous sites. Students themselves may dig into the virtual world and "find themselves" in any historical or cultural locales of the world or get acquainted with the creative biography of any renowned personality. That we all are able to easily obtain any information, "visit" any place on the globe, and communicate by electronic mail with anyone whose address we know is a great informational breakthrough. It seems as if humanity in general and the teaching/learning public in particular have patiently been waiting for this informational leap forward.

Learning about the world through the printed text and digital technologies is important. Discovering the world by seeing and "touching" it and using knowledge and impressions about what one has seen in working with students is quite another thing! Nothing can compare to people themselves exploring the world and opening for themselves new sociocultural, historical, and pedagogical frontiers. For an educator, who--as we earlier agreed--should know everything, an exploration of the world must be an important objective.

## OBJECTIVE AND SUBJECTIVE OBSTACLES

What hinders educators from seeing the world and, thus, enhancing their educational and global scope? The causal factors may include:

- lack of money to realize such plans. For decades, teachers all over the world have been reminding their governments and high ranking officials to raise their salaries. In many developing countries this problem has not shifted one bit;
- inability or lack or absence of organizational initiatives on the parts of school districts and other educational and governmental organizations to set up international grants and teacher exchange programs;
- teachers' unwillingness or reluctance to spend money on traveling owing to pursuing other incentives, for instance, the accumulation of material luxuries;
- an innate inclination to secluded life. Some educators' lives and interests are centered on the home and place they were born and

raised in; they are not given to wandering and visiting far-away places;

• an obsessive use and belief in the magical powers of the Internet and television, which can help find any possible information and knowledge about any place in the world, any personality, any pedagogical theme, and, lastly, an answer to any educational problem.

# MARVELOUS PLACES WORTH VISITING

Worldwide there are numerous amazing places worth visiting. Among them are the Sahara Desert (Africa), the Amazon Basin (South America), the Great Reef of Australia, Uluru Rock (Australia), Yosemite National Park and Muir Woods (U.S.A.), the Himalayas Mountains, Lake Ness (Scotland), and Lake Baikal (Russia). I was happy to visit some of these miraculous places and to share my insights with my students. Yosemite National Park, located in California, tremendously impacted my imagination.

Seeing the vast panorama of the Yosemite Valley, I was in awe of its natural and virgin beauty. I thought that what I was seeing was a phantom. Gradually I regained my senses and understood that this valley with its granite walls and waterfalls was a real thing. "What a spectacular masterpiece on the surface of planet earth!" I thought to myself. El Capitan, a dramatic rock wall; Half Dome, rising 4,882 feet above the valley floor; the Three Brothers rock formation, "looking" at the skies; the numerous waterfalls, looking majestically whitish and smooth from afar; the Merced River, turbulently carrying its limpid waters through the valley--all collectively represent one of nature's finest offspring.

Mesmerizing for me was standing beneath Yosemite Falls and breathing the water-saturated air. It is the highest measured waterfall in North America. El Capitan is a Mecca for climbers throughout the world. Armed with binoculars, I spotted several climbers on its marble slopes. "How do people venture to climb this, almost vertical wall"? I asked the guide who accompanied us during the tour.

"Specialists teach the volunteers climbing techniques," he said. "But they are all brave people. Of course, it is tempting, but I myself would never venture to climb this rock."

Muir Woods is another Californian wonder that made a breath-taking impression on me.

These woods represent the ancient forest having survived the tribulations of the last ice age. The Redwood Creek winding in the valley bottom attaches a special element of wilderness and, at the same time, natural beauty to the surrounding locale. Even in this "primordial" place, California presents itself as a land hospitable to people from all corners of the world. Here, too, one can encounter people speaking different languages and pursuing various religions. A middle-aged man, who happened to be German, came up to me and addressed me in broken English: "Please, picture me on tree." I understood that he wanted me to take his picture near the huge redwood tree. With pleasure I satisfied his request! He waved good-bye and continued his cognitive roaming.

Still another natural wonder that I recommend educators to visit is Lock (Lake) Ness in Scotland. I first heard about Loch Ness from my geography teacher when I was a seventh-grader.

After instructing us about the geographical situation of the United Kingdom, the teacher asked, "Who has ever heard about Lake Ness, which is in the northern part of the country, in Scotland?" With pencil in hand, she began examining the class and stopping her gaze at each learner's eyes.

Tanya, a most curious girl in our class, raised her hand. "I have read about this lake and cut a clipping with the story about the lake and Nessie, a monster inhabiting there."

"Excellent, Tanya, you have always had an eager desire to dig into interesting things."

With my hand raised and shaking, I cried from the spot looking straight at the teacher's eyes: "Please, could you tell us a little more about that lake."

The teacher told us a small but interesting story about the lake and, of course, the monster, that allegedly lived in its waters. It is the phenomenon of monster that deeply impressed me. Since then I have dreamed about going to the shore of Loch Ness in that northernmost land and trying to sight that mystical creature.

My dream came true. I literally visited the Loch Ness. When I had approached the lake near the Urquhart Castle, I suddenly felt that all the surrounding area had become mysterious and odd: the entire basin and its surface, the steep slopes, the pebble shore, the surrounding trees and bushes, the cars and tourist buses packed along the shore, and the people bustling around. It seemed that I had found myself in prehistoric times. For a time I stood terror-stricken. I could hardly keep myself from falling into the water. I even imagined that an alleged dinosaur might appear from the forest, catch someone from behind, crash his bones, and swallow him whole. Or a gigantic pterodactyl might come into sight from the opposite shore and carry some tourist away in her massive claws. I also pictured in my mind a situation how a huge water creature, probably Nessie itself, could jump out of water at lightning speed, catch someone by a leg, and take the victim to the depth.

Soon my fear and dread had vanished like smoke, and I came to my senses. Instead of a dinosaur, I saw a small boy approaching the shore, and, instead of on alleged huge prehistoric bird, two small, "21$^{st}$-century birds" were hovering above. Instead of an amphibian creature, I noticed on the surface dispersing circular rings that might have been made by small fish playing close to the surface.

I eventually lost hope of seeing a Nessie but immediately acquired a pleasurable feeling of being in a most picturesque and eminent place on earth. I received a colossal, and I should say, uncanny satisfaction from my visit to the lake. I had a time in my life!

Since the late 19th century, there have been over 10,000 sightings of a beast by different people in Loch Ness. The most famous photo was taken by Robert K. Wilson on April 19, 1934. The photo showing the neck, small head, and shoulders of a huge creature inspired enthusiasts and scientists to start searching for the strange animal.

There is a possibility that Nessie may be one of the prehistoric species (with a long life-expectancy) that could miraculously have escaped extinction and could have continued living in these mystic and deep waters. If it is so, I venture to compare their survival to that of other animal or plant species. For example, specialists theorize that the coast redwoods in California have magnificently survived evolution's upheavals, escaping annihilation during the last ice age some 20,000 years ago.

The probability of the existence of some type of unusual animal in this lake is also strengthened by the fact that the Nessie phenomenon is not unique. Throughout the world there have been reports of similar creatures in more that 250 lakes and rivers. To my mind, three probabilities may ensue from these speculations: There is no strange animal at all in Loch Ness; there is not one but a group of similar creatures; and there is only one creature that has remained after all other similar species had died.

## HISTORICAL SITES

There is a whole plethora of man-made wonders for educators to visit and deepen their professional and global horizons. These wonders, which have become the historical inheritance of humanity, include:

- the Nazca Lines (Peru) or huge drawings clearly seen only from a bird's eye-view;
- Machu Picchu (Peru), a pre-Columbian 15th-century Inca site located 7,970 feet above sea level;
- Petra (southwestern Jordan), the "Lost City" that has been featured in movies such as *Passion in the Desert, Sinbad and the Eye of the Tiger*, and *Indiana Jones and the Last Crusade*;
- Teotihuacán (the City of the Gods), located 30 miles northeast of Mexico City. It was the name of the city and the name of the civilization which lasted from 150 B.C. till 750 A.D. Some remnants of the ancient city look virtually intact;
- the Coliseum (Rome), an elliptical huge theater embodying the greatest creation of Roman engineering and architecture;
- the Taj Mahal (India), a structure the building of which was inspired by the great love of Emperor Shah Jahan for his third wife, Mumtaz Mahal;
- the Statue of Christ the Redeemer (Rio de Janeiro, Brazil). Built in 1931 and standing 130 feet high, this majestic monument endows the bay with a divine blessing;
- the Pyramids at Giza (Egypt). The questions why, how, and when they had been built have inspired passionate debate;
- Stonehenge (Great Britain). The question "How did people manage to carry the huge monoliths from so far away and build this structure?" has tortured scientists for ages;
- the Indian Ruins at Chaco Canyon (New Mexico, U.S.A.). In 900-1130 A.D., Chaco Canyon was the ancient Americans' cultural center;
- the Great Wall of China, the world's longest man-made structure stretching for 2,150 miles. It was built over 2,000 years ago;

# GREAT CITIES

The planet we live on houses a variety of spectacular human settlements that we call cities. On my lectures and seminars on global education I often show students films about the cities I appreciate most. Following are some of the cities that I advise educators to visit:

*Jerusalem (Israel).* Its history seems to be as old as the history of humanity itself. According to some estimates, it had been founded some four thousand years ago. This is a holy city to three religions: Judaism, Christianity, and Islam. Jerusalem is sacred to the Jews: It was the site of Solomon's Temple and the Second Temple. This city is sacrosanct for Christians owing to its relation to the life of Jesus Christ. Jerusalem is a divine place for Muslims, who believe that Muhammad ascended to heaven in this city.

Jerusalem has a wide range of secondary schools providing a high quality education. In the schools for Jewish children, subject areas are instructed in the native language; in addition children learn English and Arabic. In the schools with the Arabic student populations, school disciplines are taught in Arabic; in addition pupils learn Hebrew and a foreign language on a mandatory basis. At the disposal of school graduates, there are two prestigious universities: the Hebrew University of Jerusalem and Al-Quds University.

*Albuquerque (U.S.A.).* I clearly remember my first encounter with this huge sprawling settlement in the New Mexico desert.

When the plane I was in was nearing the Albuquerque International Airport, I heard someone at the back seat shouting, "Welcome to Billy the Kid's country!" It was only upon learning more about America's legendary West that I became aware of this notorious phrase. I had previously read about Billy the Kid and his outlaw career that had come to an end after Pat Garret, Sheriff of Lincoln County, had shot him dead at old Fort Summer in 1881. But I could not imagine that he might represent an American frontier symbol.

I heard this exclamation in 1994 when I arrived at Albuquerque to stay for three months as a visiting scholar at the University of New Mexico. It was my first visit to the New World, and since then I have begun opening my own pedagogical frontiers in the West. The University faculty and Albuquerque itself helped me a lot to deeply immerse into the phenomenon of multicultural education, which in the 1990s was a novel theme in my home country. After a time, in 2003, my book *Constructing*

*Multicultural Education in a Diverse Society* saw the light in the United States.

Newcomers to Albuquerque can visit the world's largest International Balloon Fiesta held annually in October; ride the 2.7-mile aerial tramway, the largest in North America; view the serpentine Rio Grand; and witness how three cultures--Native American, Hispanic, and Anglo-Saxon--harmoniously flourish in this city and in the whole of New Mexico, known as the Land of Enchantment.

*San Francisco (U.S.A.).* To my mind, this city is a *pearl* among other populous settlements of the United States. The city attracted me by its mild and foggy climate, its position on a peninsula, its architecture and numerous museums, and by its multicultural aura. I spent full six months at the University of San Francisco School of Education doing research on global education. Students from over 80 countries study at the University. In addition to fulfilling my research objectives, I explored the city, its environs, and some other spectacular places in the Golden State.

The city's outstanding landmark is Golden Gate Bridge. When it is covered with fog, only its high towers remain visible. Visiting Chinatown was a memorable experience. When I entered the Ceremonial Gate to Chinatown, the largest Chinese enclave outside Asia, I thought I found myself in China itself. One can only wonder: Its population is about 80,000 people! I and my colleague Barbara Cohen, a San-Francisco resident, could not miss an experience to enjoy a finger-licking meal at a Chinese restaurant

Another experience not to miss is riding on a cable car! I used this opportunity several times. Once, when the car was full of people, I rode *hanging on from outside*. What an experience! Other attractions are the Civic Center, Union Square, Fisherman's Wharf, and North Beach.

*Barcelona (Spain).* This settlement on the Mediterranean coast zealously keeps and values the creative legacy of the world famous Spanish architect Antoni Gaudí (1852-1926), whose works boast distinctively beautiful and incomparable shapes and styles. His magnum opus is *Sagrada Familia* (Holy Family), a Catholic church, probably the most beautiful Christian edifice in the world. Begun in 1882, it is still being built. He also designed *Casa Batlló* (Batllo House), *Casa Milà* (Mila House), *Parc Güell* (Guell Park) and other projects in this city. I was fascinated by Casa Milà, by its undulating curves on the wall and unusual artistic forms on the roof. The interior of the house is even more original in design.

Tourists also marvel at the remnants of the Roman Temple of Augustus, Catalunya Square, the Post Office Building, the Arch of Triumph, the House of Points, the National Palace, and the *Montjuïc* (Magic Fountain). I spent about an hour near the Monument to Columbus, who is said to have visited the city to share his experience with local monarchs about sailing to the New World. Columbus means a lot to the world history and *to me*, as a fervent traveler, too.

*Amsterdam (Holland).* Because of its numerous canals and merchant spirit, this city is often referred to as Northern Venice. Amsterdam's residents are tolerant, compassionate, and democratically minded. They are fond of painting. Obsessively attracted by modern styles, they do not forget their classical heritage. Deeply embedded in the Dutch heart are Rembrandt Harmenszoon van Rijn (1606-1669), Bartholomeus van der Helst (1613-1670), and Vincent Willem van Gogh (1853-1890).

Like Venice, Amsterdam is saturated by water. My dear reader! If you ever go to this city, make a boat trip on the canals. You will see the greatest attractions of its historical center and houses right on the water, in which people live permanently. Visit the Flower Market, buy a bunch of tulips. Why tulips? Because, Holland is a country of tulips!

*Prague (Czech Republic).* Receiving more than 4 million tourists annually, Prague is an incomparably beautiful city. Its historical center is included into the UNESCO list of World Historical Sites. Among the spectacular sites of the city are Prague Castle, Charles Bridge, the Jewish Quarter, Old Town, and the Lennon Wall. Two architectural masterpieces fully engrossed my imagination: the building of the National Theater and the Municipal House.

Prague houses many theaters, world class museums, cinemas, galleries, and music clubs. One can taste tens of the best sorts of Czech beer in numerous restaurants and pubs and participate in the renowned beer festival held annually in May. Education is a priority in this city, which has many universities, academies, and international institutions, including the famous Charles University, the oldest in Central and Eastern Europe.

*Saint-Petersburg (Russia).* Sprawling on the banks of the Neva River and often called the Northern Capital of Russia, it is one the most beautiful human settlements in the world. St. Isaac's Cathedral, the Winter Palace, the Academy of Arts, the Peter and Paul Fortress, the Kazan Cathedral, the Smolny Cathedral, the Yeliseyev Food Shop--all are impressive landmarks of this metropolis. The world-famous Hermitage Museum includes over three million works of art and artifacts of world culture. My favorite paintings in this museum are Leonardo da Vinci's *The Lita Madonna,* Rembrandt's *The Return of the Prodigal Son,* and Henri Matisse's *The Red Room.* There are a great variety of secondary and higher educational institution in the Northern Capital. One of them is Herzen State Pedagogical University, which prepares high-quality teachers and other specialists who work all over the Russian Federation.

How can a teacher avoid secluded existence and pursue a more active and meaningful professional and everyday life? I offer the following suggestions:

## Enhance Your Global Competency by Traveling

Do not regret when you spend money on your education, the education of your children, and on traveling. When my 14th birthday party had been over, I discovered a postcard from a relative of mine with the following note: "Do not regret spending money on education and traveling." In a year I remembered the note's content, came to a more thorough understanding of its deep essence, and made my first trip with my friend Nickolay to the city of Armavir, southern Russia. Since then I have never been forgetting this admonition.

I know many teachers and teacher educators who returned new and changed people after seeing a new place, new culture, new ways of life, and new modes of teacher-student interaction. In passing, I want to remind the reader of an episode.

After a Christmas vacation, I came to my office and noticed that all the faculty members were cheerful and full of vigor. But Tanya Gornaya was exceptionally happy and jubilant. It seemed that she was flying. Her gait was so light and gestures so flamboyant! We greeted each other and I asked, "My dear Tanya, how did you spend your Christmas?"

"Excellent, more than excellent. You know, this time, I and my husband... we visited Italy! Venice, Florence, Rome... an unforgettable trip." She raised her hands in an ecstatic gaze upwards.

I wanted to pose her a question, but she interrupted my intentions. "Oh, it was like in a dream. Right now everything is in front of my eyes! Venice is a place to visit. It is surrounded by, stands on, and pierced by, water. It is completely on water. No cars, only boats! The streets are narrow! I have never seen such streets! The canals are dark-blue. The religious shrines are majestic. We visited San Marco Square, St. Mark Basilica, and made a boat trip along the Grande Canal. In my thoughts I went back in time and formed in my mind a picture of the merchant traveler Marco Polo setting sail off Venice and of the famous painters Titian and Paolo Veronese creating their masterpieces somewhere in their Venetian studios."

I listened to Tanya's story without interrupting her. She "guided" me to Florence, Naples and other Italian cities. I grew interested in the things she was telling me. "Last year, you were in the same mood after returning from France. I hope, this time, too, you have brought some albums, postcards and other souvenirs."

"Lots of them," she said. "In due time I will tell my students and kindergarten educators about my impressions and will show them pictures." Tanya ran upstairs to her office, stopped on the landing, and looked at me. "Do you know what Rome is? It is the cradle of humanity! Marvelous!"

I saw her off with my eyes and recollected Rome, Vatican City, and other places I had seen in Italy several years before. With these nostalgic remembrances I opened the door to my office, sat at the table, and looked at the picture of Florence. "Yes," I thought to myself, "Italy is Italy!"

## Visit Other Countries

Each country is unique and worth visiting. For example, Brazil is famous for the tropical forests in the Amazon Basin and coffee; Greece, for its legendary past and the popular dance Sirtaki; Switzerland, for beautiful landscape and cheese; France, for the Eiffel Tower and good perfume; the United Kingdom, for the Beatles and tea lovers; China, for its huge population and rice; Mexico, for its ancient historical sites and sombreros; and Japan, for its people fervently pursuing their historical heritage and traditions and for good electronics.

In each country you venture to visit, you may have ample opportunities to get acquainted with the educational system face-to-face, i.e. by seeing and interacting with your foreign colleagues and students, visiting educational institutions of different types, and by witnessing how people from different ethnic and cultural background treat the issues of schooling and child development.

## Visit Local Places

You can visit natural and man-made wonders located in your own country and, probably, quite near to your residential area. It is only several years ago that I first heard about the existence of Arkaim, representing the remnants of a fortified settlement discovered by the Chelyabinsk University archeologists. The representatives of the Sintashta-Arkaim culture had lived on this site some four to five thousand year ago. This historical site is about 350 miles from the place I live. In terms of Russia's vast territory, this distance is comparable to a stone's throw from my home. After visiting Arkaim and digesting all I learned there, I became more patriotic to the Southern Urals area where my ancestors were born, enjoyed a peaceful life, and educated their kids.

## Participate in Conferences and Seminars

Participate in seminars and conferences devoted to various issues of education, child development, and to the topics related to the subject area you are teaching. With nostalgia do I remember making my first ever presentation "Enhancing students' motivation to learning a foreign language" at a teachers' seminar in Moscow. Then I was a young teacher educator. With the conference over, we all explored the historical center of Moscow. I made acquaintance with many teachers and teacher educators. I still keep a black-and-white picture with us standing against the building of the Lomonosov Moscow State University and still maintaining warm relationships with some of them.

## Show Children Your World!

"Bring the world" that you have discovered yourself to the classroom and school premises. In due time, ignite students' curiosities by providing them with the wonders of the world that you yourself saw, heard, touched, and smelled. Ensure their understanding of your world!

Reach out to students and communicate your experience in a way that is understandable and accessible to them. To enhance students' cognitive and global scope, bring and show them pictures, video fragments, albums and other interesting things and teaching materials brought from different places.

Tell them about children who belong to other cultures and about the ways how they interact with their parents and teachers.

No one objects to a good rest after a laborious and back-breaking academic year! Being away and far from students and academic noise for a month or so is what many teachers want during summer vacations. Some teachers and teacher educators are fond of a passive rest. They love spending vacations in resorts, baking in the sun, or just staying in the family circle without going anywhere.

There exists another way of spending free time--by having an active rest, when one spends vacations, weekends, and free time by becoming familiar with the world and learning more about alien cultures, customs, various historical sites as well as the ways how other peoples cope with the issues of education. I have always preferred an active form of rest and never regretted it.

Whatever occupation one is involved in and wherever one travels, one needs a language to communicate with others. What kind of language policy should we design and implement in educational institutions? How many languages should a contemporary young man and a young woman be fluent in? In the next pages I undertake a more detailed discussion of these issues.

# Chapter 6

# LANGUAGE POLICY: DOES IT EXIST?

*We are human not because we have language
but because we are language.*
Wilhelm von Humboldt

*One can only envy the peoples who, by natural reasons,
find themselves in the condition of bilingualism.*
Lev Tcherba

What kind of language policy is needed in a contemporary nation state given that the global educational space is becoming increasingly pluralistic in terms of language and ethnicity? I will try to reasonably speculate about these and related issues.

On a simple scale, the human world is distinguished from the animal world by the ability of people to converse in language--to understand other people's speech, speak, read, and to write a message. Language is an integral part of human life, a major ingredient of a reasoning entity that we call *human being*. Therefore, our world is a linguistic space in the first place.

Since our birth we easily and almost subconsciously learn to speak a language and, by the age of 6-8, we speak it relatively well. In later years we further master this language (often called--mother tongue) and in adulthood we easily communicate in it both expressively (speak it and write in it) and receptively (comprehend and understand others and read in it). So does every human being. In multilingual communities, people can acquire simultaneously more than one language.

Theorists, linguists, and language teachers have shared their amazement at the marvel of language. Meriting attention are Robert Lado's (1964) assumptions:

> When one realizes that the average human being--any normal human being--handles such a system [language] with ease, and with it the delicate sound, intonation, stress, and pause contrasts, the thousands upon thousands of words and word meanings, and he handles it all in everyday conversations and with any number of possible intentions, we are struck with wonder at the greatness of the gift of language, a gift which, among all the earthly creatures of God's creation, is given only to man. (pp. 57-58)

In a secondary school, language is both a means and aim of teaching. Language and speech as inseparable entities play a crucial role in child development, and language teachers have an important role in developing students' language and speech competency. In practice, parents, teachers instructing disciplines other than language and literature, and public at large often blame language teachers for learners' slow progress and mistakes in speech and writing. But not only language teachers but also teachers of other subject areas must help children and adolescents develop the skills of language use.

## LANGUAGE IS INSEPARABLE FROM THOUGHT

Oliver Wendell Holmes (cited in Kiplangat, 2003) describes language as "...the blood of the soul into which thoughts run and out of which they grow " (p. 1). Vygotsky (1986) assumes that thought is not only expressed in words but comes into existence through words. Marvelous and exciting considerations! Thought undergoes numerous changes before it turns into speech. The birth of verbal thought occurs as follows: from the motive engendering a thought to the molding of this thought in inner speech, then, in the meaning of words, and only afterwards, in words.

The languages people speak affect their perceptions of the world. Empirical evidence indicates that one's mother tongue molds the way one thinks about some aspects of the objective reality, including time and space (Boroditsky, 2011). For example, in the Kuuk Thaayorre language spoken in Pormpuraaw, Australia, there are no relative spatial terms such as left and right. Instead Kuuk Thaayorre speakers talk in terms of cardinal directions--east, west, north, south and so forth. English speakers take the future to be "ahead" and "past" behind. Correspondingly, they may sway their bodies forward and back. Contrarily, the Aymara speakers living in the Andes, whose body language matches their way of thinking, gesture in front of them when discussing the past and behind them talking about the future.

## THE GLOBAL LANGUAGE SITUATION

Studying the issues of education and visiting numerous educational institutions in Europe, North America, and Asia, I have with regret come to the conclusion that most of school and college graduates' language and speech literacy does not meet curriculum requirements. In the United States, teachers and faculty unanimously complain about the increasing number of errors that students of European descent commit in speaking and especially in writing in English. Some graduates of Native American origin speak their native language with accent or do not possess it at all, having totally switched to using English. Likewise, graduates of Spanish origin increasing lose touch with their mother tongue. Woodrum (2009) acknowledges that many Spanish youths (whose ancestors of direct Spanish origin settled the land in the 16-17th centuries) in New Mexico no longer speak Spanish. Like Irish- or Italian-Americans, they continue their ancestral traditions only through religious and cultural practices. During the week they work in larger cities, like Santa Fe and Albuquerque, and return to their families at weekends and holidays, which results in the loss of their native language. Native language proficiency of minority ethnic groups inhabiting European countries is somewhat similar to that of Native Americans in the United States.

Senior school teachers in Paris and Toulouse (France), Barcelona (Spain), Florence (Italy), and Emmen and Amsterdam (Holland) grumble about students' numerous speech and language mistakes in their native or principal language. Some students on the graduate level experience difficulty constructing correct sentences. They often get stuck as if in search of how to recall required vocabulary or grammar items or how to express certain idea or thought.

Most European graduates can converse in a foreign language, which is not the case across the Atlantic, in the United States, where the picture with teaching and learning foreign languages is quite different. American schools have not historically put a high priority on foreign language learning. It is estimated that only 50% of American high school students study a world language ("Going Global," 2009).

In bilingual communities people often use two languages. Bilingualism may be both natural and learned. There are also trilingual communities in the world. For instance, natural trilingualism exists among Bashkir, Chuvash, Mari, and Udmurt ethnic groups in Central Russia, who, in addition to conversing in their native tongue and Russian, can communicate, even if minimally, also in the Tatar language in the settings densely populated by Tatar people.

## A GLANCE AT THE GLOBAL LINGUISTIC SPACE

Language policies being designed and implemented in different countries are not ideal, and their contours are not as transparent as they must be. Normally, such policies defend the status and prestige of the principal or state language: In the United States young people should be fluent in English; in France, in French; in Holland, in Dutch; and in Germany, in German. Who is against learning thoroughly and being proficient in the principal or official language? Every citizen of any country is required to fluently possess the official tool of communication. But who will defend the interests of minority ethnic groups and their native languages? Who will continually remind children and adolescents of the necessity of learning at least one major foreign language?

Having discussed some important points, I now turn the readers' attention to Russia. Russia's politicians and language and education policy makers have always been responsive to the country's linguistic and ethnic mosaic and been insightful enough to understand the need for an equitable federal language policy, a policy that should involve both internal and external interests of the country. Before discussing the essence of the language policy needed in contemporary Russia and for the sake of the readers' better understanding of what Russia's secondary schools represent, I will briefly focus on the major functions that the nation's secondary schools perform and concentrate on the language situation being unfolded in this vast country.

# FUNCTIONS OF EDUCATION

Russia' secondary schools are expected to fulfill:

- an educational function. A major responsibility of secondary education is to provide students with knowledge, skills, attitudes, and values for them to productively work and live in contemporary society;
- a social function. Schools should help young people to socialize adequately and become full members of their nation state and of the world;
- the function of multicultural education, which means that all students, regardless of their ethnic, cultural, language, gender, and social class background, must have an equal and unbiased access to quality education;
- the function of citizenship education. In a contemporary society represented by ethnic and cultural diversity, citizenship education, as Banks (2004; 2009) postulates, should promote the development in students a delicate balance of cultural, national, and global identifications. These assumptions are applicable to all multicultural societies, including Russia as well;
- the function of professional orientation, which includes all necessary measures aimed at creating a transition from school to working life.

# THE LANGUAGE SITUATION IN RUSSIA

Russian is the official and principal language of the country. It is native to 82% of the population. Among other largest language groups are Tatars (4%), Ukrainians (3%), Chuvashes, Bashkirs, Belarusians, and Moldavians (1% of the entire population each), Mari, Udmurt, and Tuva. People of non-Russian ethnic descent traditionally possess both their native language and Russian and may be considered bilingual. There are also a lot of cases of trilingualism among the Bashkirs, Chuvashes, Mari, and Udmurts, as I mentioned earlier.

In ethnically and linguistically diverse areas, the language situation and quality of language education do not meet the requirements of the new epoch. A considerable number of graduates from non-Russian ethnic background, especially those finishing urban schools, are not fluent in their native language. Some of them fully lose touch with the native language and shift to exclusively using the Russian language. The graduates of non-Russian origin finishing rural schools often experience difficulty expressing themselves in Russian. While conversing orally, they have problems in pronunciation and grammar.

School graduates of Russian ethnicity, who are normally monolingual, also experience difficulties in their native language. Their weakest points are writing habits. In rural regions, Russian students' proficiency in their native language is relatively lower than that of their urban counterparts.

Exceptionally interesting is the situation with learning foreign languages. On the one hand, the issues of foreign language teaching and learning may be called unsatisfactory throughout the country. Among the many causal factors, I can name a small amount of hours and absence of societal exposure to the foreign language that children learn. In some rural and small town schools, foreign languages are not taught at all. On the other hand, there is a noticeable upsurge of motivation to learn English, even to the detriment of learning other foreign languages such as French, German, and Spanish. Many secondary schools, colleges, and higher institutions have already switched to instructing *exclusively English*.

## THE LANGUAGE POLICY

In Russia, this policy takes into account (1) the country's guideline toward language planning; (2) the ethnocultural, linguistic, and educational policies in bilingual and multilingual regions; (3) the functions and goals of secondary education; (4) the cultural and linguistic changes in Europe and in the world; and (5) the overall issues of globalization. Educators and language policy makers understand that the language policy should have the following structure and content:

- *School graduates of non-Russian ethnic background* are required to be proficient in their native language, Russian, and a foreign language. Optionally they may learn the language of another non-Russian group with the representatives of whom they come into a close contact in the corresponding autonomous republic or region. They may also learn another foreign language on an optional basis.
- *Graduates of Russian ethnic descent* should be fluent in their mother tongue, which is simultaneously the official language of Russia, a

foreign language and, also optionally, in the language of a minority ethnic group (or the language of the titular ethnic group of a certain autonomous entity) with the people of which they live in close proximity. Equally, students of Russian nationality may learn a second foreign language.

School graduates of non-Russian ethnic origin benefit from this policy in many ways. When their native language and some subject areas, such as native literature and native culture, are taught in the native tongue, there exists a high probability that the graduates acquire good habits of oral and written language and knowledge on their culture, which will instill in them a special pride and love for their indigenous land, its history, and its people. They will likely socialize easier within their close community and develop their cultural identity on a stronger basis. Proficiency in the native language is likely to help them choose a future profession in the local community, perhaps a craft or the career of the preceding generations.

Proficiency in Russian ensures the students' acquisition of knowledge, attitudes, and skills recommended by the federal curriculum, thus implementing the educational function of schooling, their socialization within a wider multicultural society, and their reflective and clarified national identifications as citizens of Russia.

Proficiency in a foreign language (especially if this language is English) is likely to provide students with newest information about the world through various mass media resources. The very process of learning a foreign language itself enhances learners' linguistic scope and masters their memory abilities. Foreign language proficiency promotes learners' global citizenship identifications and global competency, helps develop their attitudes about the world as one human society, and fosters a more lucid understanding of the essence of the present-day globalization. The ability to converse in a foreign language expands the perspectives of career orientation. Young people can find jobs in joint ventures as well as in organizations where the fluency of the target foreign language is a mandatory prerequisite.

The necessity to learn and use the language of another non-Russian ethnic group may be prompted by socioeconomic reasons, because a considerable number of young people belonging to a certain minority ethnic group work and live in the communities densely populated by the representatives of this, *another* non-Russian ethnic collective.

Learning a second foreign language may also be necessitated by socioeconomic reasons. For example, in the regions where Russia borders with

China, the ability to speak Chinese may be helpful if a graduate intends to seek a job in a Russian-Chinese joint venture.

For graduates of Russian ethnic descent, this language policy is equally beneficial. Proficiency in Russian or in their native language provides them with greater possibilities in (1) addressing their educational needs, (2) socializing within their communities and in a wider sociocultural space, (3) developing their clarified national identifications as citizens of Russia, (4) becoming multiculturally and globally competent by interacting with people from different ethnic and cultural backgrounds, and in (5) selecting their future occupations in any corner of Russia.

The ability to converse in a foreign language increases the opportunities that I mentioned while discussing the advantages of a foreign language competency for the graduates of non-Russian origin. The tendency to switch to learning English to the detriment of learning other languages proves to be consistent with the global changes sweeping all regions and continents.

Proficiency in the language of a minority ethnic group by ethnic Russians becomes important also for socioeconomic reasons. For example, in the Volga-basin autonomous republics, it becomes an asset for the people of Russian descent--especially for businessmen, medical workers, and teachers-- to converse in the titular language of the corresponding republic. Like in the case with the young people of non-Russian ethnic groups, for members of Russian ethnicity, competency in a second foreign language may be an important socioeconomic tool.

The voices echoing from different parts of the huge multicultural and multiethnic Russia evidence that young people of both non-Russian and Russian ethnic backgrounds benefit from this policy. There is also a clear understanding across the country that Russian has been the principal language on the whole territory of Russia for centuries and there is no need for selecting any second official language.

## Key Solutions

I have discussed some important issues of language situation unfolding in Russia and other regions of the world and analyzed a range of questions related to building equitable language policies. The overall situation across cultures necessitates that education and language policy makers, school district authorities, linguists, and researchers exploring sociolinguistic problems:

- carry out sociological investigations among different language groups to learn about the real state of their language literacy and proficiency;
- thoroughly investigate the issues of bilingualism and trilingualism and use their research outcomes in building beneficial language policies which meet the needs of both majority and minority groups;
- encourage secondary schools and other educational institutions to provide instruction in at least one world language;
- seek to explore the issues of language and language proficiency along with the related topics such as ethnicity and religion;
- help create in educational institutions a robust environment for all students to effectively realize their language rights;
- and design and implement unbiased language policies in their countries and regions.

It is sad but it is true: Today languages are dying faster than ever before in the world. Around 80% of all languages may become extinct in the 21st century. When a language ceases to exist somewhere in the world, it is a loss to the entire humanity (Crystal, 1997). Language is our major tool of communication and thought. *Language "makes" thought!* Why do we, then, neglect this fact?

In this chapter, among other important points, I have mentioned the English language as an important tool of communication worldwide. Is English a panacea for solving all global problems associated with international communication and can it help pave the road to establishing mutual understanding among various ethnic and cultural groups? Let us seek the answers in the upcoming section.

# Chapter 7

# WHY LEARN ENGLISH IN SPAIN AND SPANISH IN THE UNITED STATES?

*The child begins to perceive the world not only through his [or her] eyes but also through his [or her] speech.*
Lev Vygotsky

*Languages are, as we all know, subdivided into living ones and dead ones. Those who teach all languages as if they were dead are called philologists. Others, who teach living languages and who teach languages as if they were alive, are only called language teachers.*
Hugo von Hofmannstha

One of the weakest points in the American educational system is that young people of school and university age are not sufficiently motivated to learn foreign languages. This is not to say that young girls and boys do not converse in languages other than English. They do and some *succeed* in this enterprise.

We know well that times change. The contemporary epoch requires that young school and college graduates be more competent internationally and effectively function in the global cultural and socioeconomic space. Such competency requires they possess at least one world language besides English.

On the one hand, it is understandable that a U.S. citizen going abroad can do very well without being proficient in the language of the host country. English has already gained a strong international status and is being strengthened in this rank from the North to the South Pole and all along the equator. On the other hand, each ethnic and racial group boasts its own language, which is an invaluable treasure both for each of the given groups and for each individual within each group. How nice it would have been if a U.S university graduate traveling in Germany could converse in German or, when going to Italy, could communicate in Italian.

Is not it a point of pride for the representatives of an ethnic group to hear their native language spoken by a foreigner who visits their country? Each time I visited France and spoke French with French people, I noticed on their faces a feeling of excitement, satisfaction, and a little amazement from the fact that I, a Russian citizen, can talk with them in French, a language they cherish very strongly and which is a major part of their culture. In Spain I noticed the same expression on people's faces when I addressed them in Spanish.

The other side of the story is a great pride a foreigner experiences from his ability to talk in the language of the people whose country he visits. In France I spoke French, in the United Kingdom, I communicated in English. In both cases I felt myself immensely happy about my ability to address the people in their mother tongue. I was in the seventh heaven!

What I mean to say is the following: It is important to be fluent in an international language and speak it with other people when one goes to another country. This is the case when a U.S. teacher visiting Turkey can speak English with Turkish teachers. But it is also praiseworthy to be able to speak (even a bit) the language of the country one pays a visit to. This is the case when a U.S. teacher visiting Turkey can speak Turkish with Turkish colleagues.

The first case is quite typical and commonplace. The other one is atypical. And it is this latter case that may arouse a feeling of euphoria in an American teacher for his being able to converse the state language of Turkey. Likewise, it may arouse a feeling of pride in Turkish teachers for their native language because a newcomer from America *can* speak it!

First, I will substantiate my arguments about the importance of learning English in other non-English-speaking countries, including also Spain. Mentioning Spain in the title of this chapter is both symbolic and actual.

## WHY LEARN ENGLISH IN SPAIN?

Students, teachers, and public at large in Spain and other countries outside the Anglo-Saxon world are advised to possess English because it has become the language of global communication. There is more to it. Proficiency in English seems to have become a necessity for all young graduates and, also, young specialists, including those who educate and those who intend to enhance career opportunities

Whether one likes or hates it, English has become a lingua franca. For people residing in English-speaking countries, proficiency in it seems a natural part of their lives. If they all are sufficiently proficient in it or not is another question. Evidence indicates that not all residents of the United States, Canada, Australia, New Zealand, and the United Kingdom are completely proficient in this language. Similarly, not all people in Spain are completely fluent in Spanish, and not all citizens of Poland are fully competent in Polish. Simply put, it is impossible to be fully proficient in, and know all lexical and grammar details of, a language even if this language is one's mother tongue. Each of us, at any given moment of life, is only *becoming proficient* in a language.

Language is a realm so unknown that the most renowned writers use only a limited number of words and phrases in their greatest novels! So did Jack London who wrote in English, and so did Theodor Storm who put his thoughts on paper in German. What I am driving at is that all people, including also English-speaking individuals, should continually master their native language and their polyglot arsenal if they can communicate in several languages. As for the British, U.S., Canadian, and Australian citizens, they are required to show the world the best standards of oral and written speech in English, owing to its high status on the global scale. *Who else, if not them, will do it?*

The English language is "undertaking a spectacular global crusade" and penetrating into the global educational space. Beyond question, English is making inroads on the territory of European Spain. The impact of English on education and on professional and personal activities of millions of earthlings is an objective fact, and this "linguistic expansion" has resulted from natural and objective factors. Some educators in Madrid and Barcelona would have been immensely jubilant to see Spanish as an important tool of communication not only in the Caribbean and South America but throughout the world. But it is English that post-Columbian history has brought into the agenda of the 21st century.

The encroaching of English upon the planet revolving between Venus and Mars has been ignited by geopolitical, economic, and sociocultural factors. From a geopolitical perspective, this Romano-Germanic language started its world march in the 1600s. The colonial policy of the British Empire exported this language into the modern territories of the United States, Canada, Australia, and New Zealand. Later, English spread to Southeast Asia, Oceania and other regions. Competing with French in Canada, it prevailed in the number of users. From an economic perspective, English has gained an international status owing to the rise of Great Britain and, in later years, the United States and other English-speaking countries (Crystal, 1997).

Socioculturally, English has widened its global acclaim through music and movie industries. In the 1920s-1930s and post-war years, most musical events occurred in Great Britain and the United States. Young people and adults throughout the world listened and still continue listening to Little Richard, Bill Haley, Buddy Holy, Bob Dylan, Cliff Richard, Elton John, Rod Stewart, Madonna, Michael Jackson, Britney Spears, and Alicia Keys. A considerable number of people on all continents, especially teenagers and young adults, appreciate the pop groups such as the Beatles, the Rolling Stones, the Who, Creedence Clearwater Revival, the Eagles, Smokie, U2, and Nirvana.

In addition, a wide range of singers and groups in non-English-speaking countries rose to fame largely by performing in English. Among them were the Jamaican group Boney M and singer Bob Marley, the Swedish group ABBA, and the German group Modern Talking. The Columbian singer-songwriter Shakira's fame was largely instigated when she had started singing in English. In reflecting on popular music, especially rock-and roll, I cannot hold myself aloof and want to confess that I was and am a fan of both popular and classical music.

To popular music I include all genres or combination of styles such as rock-and-roll (in the first place), rap, blues, reggae, etc. To be exact, I love *my* pop. What does this signify? First of all, I prefer listening to what appeals to me most. What stirs and arouses my heart and soul most is a touch of an attractively *mild huskiness* in a singer's voice, which is peculiar, for example, to Chris Norman and Rod Stewart. When I first heard Chris Norman's singing the huge hits such as *Don't Play Your Rock'n'Roll to Me* and *Wild, Wild Angels,* it struck me as if I had been waiting for a long time for this sounding matter and, at last, it had arrived. It seemed to me as if these songs *had been addressed to me.* Rod Stewart's *Sailing* and *Rhythm of my Heart* aroused similar feelings.

As for classical music, I am also selective and love listening to *my* favorites from different composers such as Wolfgang Amadeus Mozart, Ludwig van Beethoven, Pyotr Tchaikovsky, Nikolai Rimsky-Korsakov, Dmitri Shostakovich, and George Benjamin. Vivid in my mind is my visit to Mozart's hometown Salzburg in Austria. Unmistakably, Salzburg is Mozart's city. Mozart is an omnipresent phenomenon in the city. Sometimes it even becomes unclear whether Mozart is Salzburg's greatest offspring or this baroque city is an offspring of Mozart. Many things are related to, and associated with, this musician who created over 600 compositions including chamber music, concertos, and symphonies. One of his spectacular creations is *The Marriage of Figaro*, an opera that I am especially fond of. My favorite ballet is Tchaikovsky's *Swan Lake*.

Movie industry has also largely fostered the spreading of English across the world. Since the 1920s, English has become the dominating language in cinematography. In the 1930s, among the existing 44 movie studios, 32 were in the United States and Great Britain; 318 out of 340 producers used English in their movies (Crystal, 1997).

The current global status of English can be substantiated by several facts (Sinagatullin, 2009a). First, it is the most widely distributed language in the world: It has an official status in more than 50 countries. Besides, a considerable number of people in the countries where English is not official can converse in it with a reasonable degree of proficiency. Second, there is a growing motivation among young people in the world to learn this means of communication. Millions of young girls and boys learn English at schools and colleges, others learn it out of necessity for furthering a career, and still others learn it for the prestige that it might bring to them. In many non-English-speaking countries, educational institutions, ranging from kindergartens to schools and universities, have replaced other foreign languages by switching to teaching English.

Third, English is increasingly used in written, electronic, and satellite communication. It is often used as the major working language in international seminars, conferences, and symposiums. Most scientific publications throughout the world see the light in English. The popularity of it has enormously increased owing to the development of the Internet and other means of high-speed communication. Fourth, acquiring specific pronunciation modifications and coloring, many English words and phrases have made their way into the active vocabulary of many peoples. The language units such as *hi, wow, hello, I love you, music, no problem, baby, drink, boyfriend, money, good bye* and others are used on a daily basis across the globe.

Fifth, English language proficiency opens new avenues for educators and learning public. They can participate and interact with their colleagues in international research and exchange programs organized in English-speaking and other countries. For example, the Fulbright Program, established in 1946 by the U.S Congress, is one of the most well-known programs providing awards to students, educators, scholars, and researchers in the United States and other countries. In Germany, the *Deutscher Akademischer Austausch Dienst* (German Academic Exchange Service) provides scholarships for foreign students and academics, educational cooperation for developing countries, and university courses leading to an international degree.

Sixth, English promotes the creation and strengthening of a common global educational space. It spreads across all continents, seas, and oceans; fosters reorganizations in the educational systems of different countries; and increases the exchange of students, faculty, and scholars. Even though symbolic in nature today, some day the notion of *global educational space* may be officially endorsed if governments and high ranking educational structures come to a mutual understanding that education is a highest priority in human society and that the overall goals of education and child development have much in common in all cultures, regardless of their ethnic, ideological, religious, and linguistic makeup.

There is hardly any evidence to suggest that English as a global language will be replaced with any other language in the years to come (Sinagatullin, 2009a). What we see now is the following:

> The English language is roaming on sea, land and air. It is transmitted with the speed of lightning, and its melodic vowels and resilient consonants are heard in the remotest and isolated places.... Will its fate repeat that of Latin, now extinct in its oral form, or that of Sanskrit that we frequently mention in the linguistic literature as a flourishing language in the days of yore, or will it mix up with other languages and grow into diverse Creole ramifications in the years to come? To this question, we do not know the exact and plausible answer. For the time being, across the seven continents, a growing number of people involved in the business of education and research communicate and gain newest information and knowledge by means of this language. To me, a person natively speaking a language other than English, it only remains to thank God and fate for granting me an opportunity and possibility to reflect the objective reality by using this letter-and-sound system of communication. (p. 310)

## WHY LEARN SPANISH IN THE UNITED STATES?

Around 500 million people in the world converse in Spanish. A mind-staggering figure! It is the official language in almost all countries of Latin

America. People in Mexico, Colombia, Venezuela, Peru, Bolivia and many other countries communicate in this language. The United States' borders are in close proximity to Latin America. Spanish flourishes on the same continent as the United States. We often call this continent by one name--*America!* In the international communication, Spanish is the second most used language ("Learning Spanish," 2006).

The Spanish-speaking population is distributed in the following way: North America--154,276,438 million speakers; Central America--40,982,389; South America--191,225,429; Europe--40,491,051; and Islands--24,889,213 speakers ("World Spanish," 2009). The Hispanic population in the United States and the Hispanic world is growing rapidly. By 2150, the population in Latin America and the Caribbean may reach 8,6 billion people (Rimashevskaya, 2002a). In 2008, 44,321,038 million people in the United States were Spanish-speaking, thus making this nation the third Spanish-speaking country (after Mexico--109,955,400 million people and Colombia--45,013,674) in the world. The U.S. Hispanic population may constitute 29% of the nation's population by 2050 (Nasser, 2008). With an average-level of Spanish language proficiency, students, educators, and university faculty can travel around a huge part of the world and, without embarrassment, communicate with 500 million people across the globe. The rapid growth of the Hispanic population in the United States has increased the demand for Spanish mass media.

In the United States, Spanish is growing as a business language in addition to English and provides more employment opportunities both to Hispanic and non-Hispanic people. In southern United States, especially in Arizona, New Mexico, Texas, and Florida, Spanish is a widely used language. As Spanish is making strides in this function, the ability to converse both in English and Spanish becomes an economic and cultural necessity. Therefore, in these regions, not only Hispanics should be proficient in English, but also people of Anglo-Saxon descent are expected to be fluent in Spanish.

The Spanish were the first Europeans to come to the Americas as permanent settlers after Christopher Columbus had "discovered" it in 1492. Mexico was conquered in 1519-1521 by Hernando Cortés and Peru in 1532 by Francisco Pizarro. Latin culture has been making a global impact on art and literature. We are all familiar with *Don Quijote de la Mancha* by Miguel de Cervantes and have enjoyed viewing Picasso's masterpieces. The movie stars Antonio Banderas and Penélope Cruz and singers Ricky Martin, Enrique Iglesias, Gloria Estefan, and Shakira are all the representatives of Latin culture. Latin American countries show strong economic growth, making them important commercial partners of the United States.

Why is it so important for young Americans of non-Spanish origin to learn Spanish? The Spanish language is:

- a densely distributed tool of communication in the Caribbean and South America, the regions with which the United States sustains favorable academic, cultural, and economic ties;
- native to a large percent of U.S. population;
- a business language in most of the southern parts of the country;
- a vital part of Spanish culture that has historically made a paramount impact on the development of the United States according to the principle *E Pluribus Unum*.

An episode from my life has interesting associations with the American frontier times when the Spanish were exploring and settling what we call now southwestern United States.

I remember standing on a road parallel to Rio Grand in Albuquerque, New Mexico, when my colleague, a school teacher, pointed to the road and said: "You are standing on the former historical road *El Camino Real de Tierra Adentro Trail*, first traveled by Don Juan de Oñate in 1598." Then, I paid no particular attention to what the colleague had said. It is only after digging in the Internet and other sources that I understood that this route, extending from Mexico City to San Juan Pueblo, New Mexico, had been the Spanish colonial royal road or the Royal Road of the Interior Land from 1598 until 1882.

Days later I returned and walked some distance along this trail, imagining how people, on foot, on horseback, and on horse- and ox-drawn carriages, had slowly headed in both directions--northwards and southwards. For those people, their geological epoch and time should have been the zenith of human and technological progress and Spanish represented the most important means of interpersonal and international communication. Those travelers and settlers had not been mistaken to take Spanish as being such a language in those days. Spanish had been a great language *in those* frontier days and has boasted such a status *since those* times.

# WHY LEARN FRENCH IN THE UNITED STATES?

Used by over 200 millions of people worldwide, French is one of the official languages in certain regions of multilingual countries: in Belgium (Wallonie region), Canada (Québec province), and in Switzerland (Jura, Genève, Neuchâtel, and Vand districts). In many countries French has an important role, either as an administrative, commercial, and international language or due to a significant French-speaking population. According to Laura Lawless (2012), such countries reach 26 in number, including the United States, where French is not a forgotten language in Louisiana and New England. There are around 68 millions of people in the world who speak French as their first language or mother tongue (Janssen, 2011). It is the official language of the UN, UNESCO, the International Olympic Committee, the European Union, and the International Red Cross. As a foreign language, it is the second most frequently taught language in the world after English.

France and the French language have historically had a huge influence on American culture. Many of the most important writings in the humanities and social sciences came from France. Americans and people in other countries remember the creative talent of the philosopher and pedagogue Jean-Jacques Rousseau (1712-1778); novelist Alexandre Dumas père (1802-1870); political scientist Alexis de Tocqueville (1805-1859), who wrote the best-seller *Democracy in America*; and singer Édith Piaf (1915-1963). From a historical perspective, France has been known to the world public as a center of learning and education. The French are also known as skillful movie makers and as recognized cosmetics manufacturers. The United States is a leading investor in France. Canada, where French is spoken along with English, is its largest trading partner.

Americans remember well that the Statue of Liberty was a gift from France to the United States.

> Several times I saw this statue from the air on the Liberty Island in New York Harbor. I know from my school textbooks that the idea to rise this sculpture was announced by the French politician Edouard René de Laboulaye in 1865 and that the French engineer Alexandre-Gustave Eiffel designed the iron carcass of the statue.
>
> Eiffel's engineering genius constructed many other edifices and structures. Among them is the 1,063-foot tall Eiffel Tower in Paris. I was in cloud nine in the direct and figurative senses of the word when, with my wife Zemfira, I climbed this 19th-century skyscraper, a cultural icon

of Paris and the whole France. Atop the edifice, Zemfira suddenly said, "Now I can breathe freely and say confidently that I *have* visited Paris and France!" I looked downwards from the dizzy and intoxicating height and added loudly, "Wow, me, too, without doubt!"

In sum, the reasons to learn French for U.S. school graduates are the following. The French language is:

- a widely distributed language across the globe and the official language in a wide range of countries;
- the official language of Canada, with which the U.S.A. maintains tight educational, sociocultural, and economic links;
- the official language of France, whose culture has been and is still making a significant influence on American culture and styles of life.

## WHY LEARN ITALIAN IN THE UNITED STATES?

The reasons for this are obvious and many. First, Italian is a highly distributed language across the world and spoken as a mother tongue by 65 million people. Italian and Italian dialects are widely used by Italian immigrants and their descendents in the northern European countries, Canada, the United States, Australia, Uruguay, Brazil, and Venezuela. The total number of Italian speakers in the world is over 85 million ("Italian language," 2011). Second, the United States has considerable Italian-speaking populations in Boston, New York, Philadelphia, Chicago, and Miami, where Italian is frequently used as a business language. Third, Italian culture has had a strong influence on European and American cultures.

Fourth, Italy lies on the site of the former great Roman civilization, the achievements of which still affect, overtly or covertly, the shaping of Western civilization, with the United States being part of it. In the Western world and partly in other regions, Roman influence is noticeable in arts, literature, law, city-planning, and in the organization of democratic government practices. Roman influence can be seen in road-building and architecture. English and other Western languages, including Italian, have been developed from Latin, the official language of Rome. The greatest writers have been influenced by Roman life and by the very idea of *romanness*: William Shakespeare wrote *Anthony and Cleopatra* and *Julius Caesar* and Dante created *Inferno*.

My first visit to Rome, the capital city of Italy, occurred after I had already visited Washington; and it was in Rome that I discovered for myself two visible connections between the ancient Rome and contemporary Washington. While roaming about the remnants of the Roman Forum, investigating the surviving columns of the Temple of Saturn and the Temple of Venus and Roma, and marveling at the Forum and Markets of Trajan, I immediately brought to mind the buildings of the Supreme Court, the National Portrait Gallery, and of the Capitol (from the back side) in Washington. The resemblance between the architectural style of ancient Rome and that of some major edifices of Washington was breath-taking.

But when I approached the Pantheon, Rome's only intact monument from classical time, goose pimples stood out on my skin, because it suddenly struck me that I was standing in front of the central part of the building of the National Gallery of Art in Washington. This time, the resemblance of the edifice built in 27 B.C. and the building constructed in 1941 was not only breath-taking but hair-raising.

Another connection that I noticed is embedded in the technology and the very spirit of road building. It is universally known that Roman roads were--and some of them still are--solid and long-lasting. They were paved with large fitted stones lain upon a foundation of rock. I proved it by touching the stones of *Via Sacra* (Sacred Road), the main road and street through the Forum. The same spirit and responsibility are felt when one drives along American highways. They are firm, durable, and play a vital role in enhancing the nation's economy and overall sociocultural infrastructure. They are the arteries of the United States. Like ancient Roman roads, contemporary American roads represent a great engineering accomplishment.

## WHY LEARN RUSSIAN IN THE UNITED STATES?

The Russian language is native to 80% of Russia's entire population and to many people living now on the territories of the former Soviet Union. It is the first language of 144 million people across the world (Janssen, 2011), the most widely spoken of the Slavic languages and a language of international communication on the post-Communist space. Russian speaking populations live in the United States, Germany, Israel, Australia and other countries. All in all, Russian-speaking people live in 140 countries.

Russian immigrants have been settling on the territory of the United States for more than a hundred years. The Russian population in many parts of the United States is increasing. I heard Russian spoken on the Miami South Beach, in the streets of downtown San Francisco, and even in the valley of Yosemite National Park in California. By the manner of carrying themselves in American society and by the specificities of their pronunciation, the speech I heard belonged not to Russian tourists who had come on a short visit but to people of Russian origin who should have lived in the country for long while and possibly received the American citizenship.

Russian-born writers Leo Tolstoy (1828-1910), Anton Chekhov (1860-1904), Fyodor Dostoevsky (1821-1881), Mikhail Bulgakov (1891-1940), Vladimir Nabokov (1899-1977); chemist Dmitry Mendeleev (1834-1907); physiologist Ivan Pavlov (1849-1936); and pedagogue and psychologist Lev Vygotsky (1896-1834) have exerted powerful influence on shaping Americans' humanitarian and educational thought.

The Soviet Union's spectacular breakthrough into space by launching the first Sputnik satellite in 1957 and the spaceship with Yuri Gagarin aboard in 1961 spurred increases in U.S. science education funds and, simultaneously, instigated and expedited the space exploration programs and the programs of developing the potential of gifted and talented children.

The Russian language is gaining momentum in the United States and other countries on the American continent because:

- it is a widely distributed language in Eurasia and its speakers are on the increase in other parts of the world, including the U.S.A.;
- Russia has embarked on the track of democracy and market economy and is entering the global educational space, which confirms that she is on the way of stable development. Strengthening socioeconomic and educational cooperation with Russia will pay off in many ways to the United States and the rest of the Western world.

## IMPORTANT SOLUTIONS

The preceding discussion thus far leads to some implications. The current epoch requires that education policy makers, school district officials, and school administrators:

- have a transparent understanding of the following fact: Along with other measures, an important task in conceptualizing and implementing a language policy in a country involves teaching to young people one or more world languages;
- impress on educators and parents that, among other internationally acclaimed languages, English has come to the forefront as an important tool of communication. Other globally and regionally widespread languages are Spanish, French, Russian, German, Chinese, Arabic, and Portuguese;
- understand that, even though English is natively spoken in the Anglo-Saxon countries and is the official language in many other countries, and that the residents of English-speaking countries can do without possessing the native language of a country they plan to visit, nevertheless, the residents of English-speaking countries, in any case, are expected and should learn foreign languages. School district officials and school administrators in the United States and in the English-speaking world are required to pay a greater attention and exert more effort to motivate students to learn foreign languages.

Years ago a wise person said, "We can take man as being man as many times as the number of languages he possesses." This whimsical saying has a touch of humor in it; but each humor or joke is known to incorporate a quota of truth. With this "serious joke" I end this chapter in order to start discussing another one devoted to the children who are fate-offended and the overlooked victims of our reasoning civilization. The fates of such children does not always depend on *what* language they speak but, predominantly, on *how* we speak with them.

*Chapter 8*

# NEGLECTING THE UNLOVED

*Suppose one of you has a hundred sheep and loses one of them...*
*When he finds it,...he says, 'Rejoice with me; I have found my lost sheep.'*
Luke 15:4-6.

*When love and skill go together, expect a masterpiece*
John Ruskin

The title of the chapter embraces two negative connotations. The verb *neglect* encompasses the meaning of being indifferent toward something. The term *unloved* contains the idea of being neglected, underestimated, and overlooked. One can only imagine what a sad situation may unfold when a human being who has been unloved for years--due to his physical or mental disability, misbehavior, or low grades at school--is, in addition to all these troubles, also neglected, kept at a distance, and marginalized by the teaching personnel and students.

To more coherently explain the point I am driving at, first, I will point out the most important types of the organization of schooling.

## TYPES OF EDUCATION

- *Authoritarian Education.* It is based on harsh principles of teaching, strict discipline, and on obedience in class and school premises. As a rule, authoritarian education is characteristic of countries adhering to one dominant ideology or religion. However, an authoritarian style of

educating the young may be peculiar to certain teachers in any
society.

- *Educational Progressivism.* Progressive education programs focus on
  learning by doing and on strong emphasis on problem solving and
  critical thinking. Emerging in the 19th century, this pedagogical
  movement has persisted to the present day.

- *Religious Education.* Such an education seeks to provide individuals
  with beliefs and rituals of a particular religion. For instance, in the
  United States, religious education is provided through Sunday school,
  Hebrew school, catechism classes and so forth. Endorsing a religion at
  a public school infringes the First Amendment to the Constitution
  ("Religious Education," 2012).

- *Military Education.* It provides enlisted individuals with knowledge,
  values, and skills that prove invaluable in subsequent conditions.
  Military education, which may be compulsory or voluntary, is
  provided in different institutions including military academies. Their
  exact definitions depend on the country concerned.

- *Home Schooling.* Providing alternative educational solutions, home
  education provides both potential benefits and responsibilities. Home
  schooling allows parents to provide their children with the
  opportunities to educate them at home. Parents themselves or special
  tutors can play the role of teachers and educators. Several home
  schooling families may create a group of home schooled children to
  organize and participate together in a variety of educational and social
  activities.

- *Democratic Education.* There are countless definitions given by
  theorists and working pedagogues to explain the phenomenon of
  democratic education. To my mind, such an education should be
  based on democratic principles and laws, and both learners and
  teachers should be equal participants of the two-way pedagogical
  process. Not all educators fully understand the true nature of
  democracy and how to implement it in working with children. This
  lack of understanding is a major problem with the wholehearted
  implementation of democratic education.

- *Nonviolence Education.* Such an education fully rejects violence and
  aggression and appeals to teachers and parents to resolve all
  difficulties in child-adult relationships in a humane and constructive
  way. The ideas of nonviolence education stem from the founding
  principles proposed by Jean-Jacques Rousseau and Mahatma Gandhi.

It appears that authoritarian education, rigid as it is, blazes a trail to academic success; progressive education deals with developing children's creativity; religious education ensures young people's understanding of important spiritual canons of life; military education prepares the growing generations to be strong and, if necessary, to defend their homeland; an education organized at home seeks to provide a learning environment competitive to that in a public school; democratic education focuses on the idea of equal participation of both teachers and students in the teaching/learning process; and nonviolence education calls teachers to realize humanistic goals of teacher-students interaction.

These are the so-called "well-adopted" forms of educating the young. Nevertheless, these and other types of education contain propitious possibilities and unique loopholes permitting educators to love some part of learners and to feel a dislike for the other part.

## WHO ARE THE LOVED?

From a purely earthly perspective, an average human being tends to prefer the sweet to the sour, the beautiful to the ugly, and a warmer climate to a colder one. This trend, which can be easily explained in a normal day-to-day situation, is often "transferred" to the realm of education. How can we notice it in reality? Pedagogical reality manifests this trend by the fact that some educators are more favorably disposed and have a more nurturing attitude to girls and boys who behave properly in class and school milieu, progress academically, actively volunteer to participate in classroom discussions, participate in extracurricular and social activities, obey the teachers' requirements and orders, and who look more beautiful or more handsome. Educators may have a better disposition to learners who have affluent or respected parents or relatives who are related to, or neighbors of, the educator. Educators tend to pay more attention to physically healthy and socio-emotionally well-balanced children or to those who appeal to them for various subjective reasons. All the mentioned categories of children are those whom all or almost all people love or pay respect due to natural, objective reasons.

While visiting lessons of both pre- and in-service teachers, I noticed one "strong tendency" prevalent in our profession. Student teachers and working teachers tend to ask more and interact more with brighter students who "help educators out of a difficulty" when someone else is visiting a lesson and sitting on the back row. Teachers seem hesitant to ask low-achieving learners because they may let the teacher down in front of the visitor.

Now, I guess the reader has started to understand more deeply what I meant by saying "neglecting the unloved." I meant one thing: By their natural and physical instincts, educators pay more attention to those *who are already loved and respected* and tend to have a less affection and love toward nature-, fate- and society-offended children. i.e. to those *who are already less noticed and receive less nurturing.* As a result, these "already loved" and "already respected" children are likely to receive even more adoration and a greater sense of attachment from educators than the children who are already less noticed.

## WHO ARE THE UNLOVED?

And who are the unloved children? They are children who are on the other side of the continuum. They are low-achievers academically, tend to disrupt the norms of good order in class and elsewhere, escape social activities, disregard teachers' requirements, and look less pretty and less handsome. These are children from poor, one-parent, and parentless families and children with alternative physical and mental health. These are kids who fall out from the list of students that we traditionally call *normal.*

What kind of children and adolescents can be referred to as being less noticed, less favored and, ultimately, less loved? I will provide some of my considerations on these issues in more detail.

*Parentless and Abandoned Children.* I myself was born and raised in a full family. My father, who died at the age of 78, incessantly loved me and my mother, who is 84 at the time when the book goes to press, loves me now. My sister had died at a young age, prior to my birth. I have received full affection since the time I was born and have always been conscious that some other children have been less fortunate, because they have not been enjoying the luxuries I and other people like me take for granted.

In modern pedagogy, not only parentless children but also those abandoned by their parents are often rendered as orphans. Governments and local authorities do a lot to provide orphans with affection, care, education, and medical treatment by placing them in children's homes or undertaking other measures. However, problems are many and they are varied, and not all children whose parents have died find refuge in orphanages. A considerable number of school-age children throughout the world have to drag out a miserable existence. They have to endure cold weather; hunger; physical, psychological, and sexual abuse; and they have to sleep in street and square corners, cellars, attics, trenches, and under bridges. On the one hand, the human civilization is harmoniously moving to novel heights; on the other, the number of orphaned children has risen across the continents, with the AIDS pandemic being the greatest "contributor." On a sharp increase is the number of AIDS orphans in Sub-Saharan Africa.

Owing to the fact that my wife worked at a children's home for 18 years, I have come to learn a lot about what joys and sorrows parentless and abandoned children experience. I and my wife used to take their psychological and social difficulties to heart. I remember her bringing to our house some of the girls and boys to explain difficult academic material to them. At other times, they shared with us dinners and holiday parties in our house or garden. I came to know that some children, even if they had one or both parents, did not want to return to their parental homes in which alcohol abuse had become a seven-days-a-week and twelve-months-a-year practice. Some did not want to pay even a brief visit to their family circle. For them, their former life with drinking parents resembled a nightmare they did not want to have again.

*Children from Poor Families.* It is sad to acknowledge but prosperity and poverty have always dwelled side-by-side in societies, ranging from ancient sedentary communities in Turkish Anatolia to the Roman Empire and on to the contemporary European countries and the United States. In almost all cities we call beautiful and spectacular, like San Francisco and Moscow, one can encounter whole clusters of poverty-stricken and homeless people of different ages, who often compose some informal, close-knit communities of their own.

The causes leading to family and child poverty are myriad, complex, and diverse. Low income of parents, family structure changes, no-parents-in-the-labor-force families, single-parent families, disorganized families (when one or both parents are alcoholics or drug addicts)--all these and other unfavorable conditions may result in poverty among children and teenagers.

Poverty causes instability and insecurity for everyone in human society. The phenomenon of poverty and children's physical, socioemotional and cognitive development are closely interrelated. Children living in low-income families are more likely to have educational and health problems and to experience parental divorce than the children who live in well-off and affluent families. Every year a great number of children slip into the relentless tentacles of poverty. Poverty is like slavery. Not without reason, in 1995, Juan Somavia (Barr, 1995) challenged the members of the Canadian Council for

International Cooperation to do for poverty what abolitionists did for slavery--to create a new movement whose goal must be the elimination of poverty.

We all know well that a child needs the care of both parents. Unfortunately, different circumstances leave children with one parent. Divorce is a tragedy many families experience these days. Left with a mother, a child is at a substantially higher risk of economic and psychological problems. Children in single-mother homes are more likely to experience academic (lower level of education, higher absentee rates at school) and behavior (higher probability of delinquent activity) problems. The lack of a male income continually worsens the overall situation in single-mother families. I have no intention to diminish the role of mothers in child development, but fathers' share in child development is not less important. Positive father involvement provides children with guidance, support, and *paternal love* that is specific in its nature and essence.

In the communities and areas with a high level of crime, there is a higher probability that family members may be victims of crime. When a father is imprisoned, the consequences for a mother and her children may be devastating. A child whose farther is incarcerated is more likely to resort to antisocial behavior, lag behind in school, marry at an early age, and to abuse alcohol or drugs. Children growing with one parent (the other being incarcerated) have a stronger likelihood to experience poverty and hunger. When the breadwinner in the family is incarcerated, the remaining parent and children have a stronger likelihood to lead a beggarly existence.

*Children with Alternative Behavior.* No matter how effective the ways of teacher-student interaction are, some children will break the required academic and social norms. Children's disruptive behavior is caused by numerous factors. Whoever they are, educators, parents or other people responsible for child development are morally obliged to put a child right, either pinpointing the root cause of a misbehavior or tolerantly working to discipline the child by using all possible means and approaches.

*Rural Children.* Evidence suggests that rural children and adolescents are often marginalized. There are two reasons for this. First, there exists a hard-to-eradiate tradition among urban dwellers to diminish anything related to rural life. This long-standing belief "spreads its tentacles" over and contaminates all human societies and social infrastructures including the issues of teaching and child development. For example, rural learners may be put into the "position of less importance" when they move to urban schools from their former rural schools. Who puts them into this position? Their urban peers and, sometimes, urban educators themselves.

Second, in multiethnic and multilingual rural communities, children from numerically smaller ethnic groups traditionally converse both in their native and dominant (official) languages, but they are more exposed to communicating in the former. The closure or consolidation of rural schools make some rural families move to urban areas. When they move to urban areas to continue their education, some of these newly arrived students start experiencing difficulty conversing in the official language and have to overcome serious linguistic barriers to become "equal" to their (urban) peers. For example, in Russia, the Bashkir and Tatar children who live in rural communities are bilingual: They are exposed to both Tatar and Russian. As they predominantly communicate in Tatar, their skills in speaking and writing in Russian are not as proficient as those in Tatar. Some students have a phonetic accent while conversing in Russian; others may commit lexical, grammar, and stylistic mistakes in oral and written speech.

*Gifted Children.* Paradoxical as it may sound, sometimes talented and gifted students also remain less noticed and, eventually, less loved under the pretence that they can cope with academic and other problems *by themselves,* without educators' and parents' assistance. Left to the "mercy of fate," they may literally "start developing by themselves," blazing "their own trails" in exploring the world. Such method of self-control and self-regulation may lead to unpredictable outcomes.

# "UGLY" AND "UNATTRACTIVE" CHILDREN

Historically, the phenomena of being attractive or unattractive (in both physical and spiritual sense) have been one of the most visible traits, yet their true essence may have never been fully explained. A person may attract others by his or her manner of communication, decent behavior, the ability to prepare a good meal, the ability to perform a certain job properly, by being a good painter, or just by being pretty. There exists a more or less "commonly accepted opinion" that less attractive individuals (both males and females) have fewer advantages in life and in human relationships than more attractive people.

Among other things related to attractiveness, physical attractiveness is the most intriguing and most enchanting category. In adults, physical attractiveness is often associated with sexual attractiveness. It is impossible to conceal the fact that people who are less beautiful in appearance tend to have less choice in romantic partners and to receive less attention from other people. People attribute positive characteristics to attractive people even without consciously realizing it. Generally, men value physical attractiveness more than women ("Physical attractiveness," 2012).

In the teaching profession the attitude of educators to the overall phenomenon of attractiveness/unattractiveness somewhat repeats, with specific variations, the "well-established" historical trend. As if "imitating this trend," educators also tend to rate attractive children more favorably than unattractive ones (Jordan, 1975). Some teachers view physically attractive children as possessing higher intellectual ability and more socially acceptable and desirable behavior (Richman, 1978). As a teacher educator, I do not intend to dramatically change human history, but the issues surrounding this phenomenon *need to be changed* in the domain of education and parent-child relationships.

With all these assumptions in mind, I encourage educators to listen to the following suggestions:

## Manifest a Stronger Love to the Marginalized and Unloved Children

Your love for children should be sincere and strong. But your love for the unloved must be even stronger than that for the rest of the class or group. It should be even more sacrificial. The unloved need unconditional love and full acceptance. Your attitude and love should not depend on a student's manner of behavior and academic achievement. When it comes to teaching and child rearing, loving the unloved is a most vital and humanistic quality.

Avoid stereotyping children into the achievers and non-achievers, the normal and abnormal, the beautiful and modest, and into my child and other people's children. All children are on the same ladder. Some have climbed a little bit higher, others are several rungs lower. You should help by all possible means the latter to reach higher level.

## Be Sensitive to Students from Low-Income Families

Low-income families are not always able to provide their children with all necessary assets that a contemporary growing child needs. Many school graduates from low-income and large families are unable to actualize their dreams to enter a college or university and have to join the workforce. Others are compelled to pick any job to make ends meet.

Be especially tolerant and sensitive to children living in poverty and straitened circumstances. Contact social and charity organizations in working with poverty-stricken children. All school personnel are required to create for them safe and healthy academic conditions and give them a chance to grow into productive adulthood.

Students from low-income and vulnerable families and from immigrant minority groups need the school and district authorities to offer them favorable conditions such as reduced prices for buying necessary learning aids, computers, textbooks, for using public transportation, and for meals.

## Provide a Cordial Environment for Orphans

In your class there may be orphans who live in children's homes, orphanages, or similar institutions. Provide such children with love and care. Collaborate with the medical personnel, psychologists, and social pedagogues in providing them with a required medical care and advice and in teaching them the skills of interaction in a wider society.

Some orphans are given shelter by their relatives and other families. Get to know such families and collaborate with them in finding optimal approaches to provide the necessary nurturing. You may also work with people who volunteer to take care of the children to whom fate has dealt a cruel blow. In dealing with orphans, emphasize the use of both institutional and community-based care. In other cases just *be a mother* to orphans and other fate-offended children and deal with them as with your own children.

One of the most difficult problems for orphans and, in fact, for other children who live in children's homes is the transition to adult life after their graduation from secondary school. Even though local authorities monitor this process, in reality some adolescents are not able to cope with this transition. Monitor their transition from childhood to adulthood. As in other cases, in this case too, it is necessary to work out collective efforts to help them socialize and favorably step onto the path of independent life. Empower them with a hope for a brighter future.

## Be a Positive Role Model for Children

Children and adolescents are known to imitate educators' ways of behavior, their modes of interaction with colleagues and students, their strategies of teaching, manners of greeting, various gestures, and their styles of clothing. The child nurturing process has an *exemplary nature*; therefore educators have to be especially attentive to themselves. This slogan is important for all educators and in all educational and child-rearing institutions as well as for all parents and adults involved in frequent interactions with the young.

But this slogan becomes twice as important in interacting with children who lack positive role models in a children's home, an orphanage, and in their families. In such cases educators are the only individuals who *can and should* show appropriate manners. For this reason, be a positive role model for your students in class, on the school grounds, and in the outer society. If you work in a village or small town school, you should be even more cautious about your manners of interaction with parents and community members, because in such conditions you are viewed by everybody.

## Love Each Pupil as Your Own Child

To love a child means many things. It may denote that we should forgive them, treat them on an equal and unbiased basis, be tolerant and compassionate in dealing with them, create a healthy and robust psychological climate in class, exert an empathetic attitude toward them, and be able to attentively listen to and trust them. These are all effective pedagogical methods and approaches, and educators should exhibit them in corresponding circumstances. But the truth is that each of these approaches can only partially solve the entire spectrum and the long-term goals of child development.

Whatever approach, strategy, or instructional style an educator probes and uses and whatever type of education we implement, a favorable solving of the process of child development inevitably runs into psychological barriers between the notions of "my own child" and "someone else's child."

Rethink and overcome this barrier and start loving and treating each child in your class as *your own child*. The art of cherishing each child as your own offspring is so facile and, simultaneously, so complicated, but the very course of it, even though it may require sacrifices, is so divine and so heavenly. Even though such a pure love in its ideal form may not exist in your heart now and the very notion of it may sound otherworldly, step onto the path of solving this glorious task and strive to fulfill it in small increments.

It is very easy to love a child who is academically advanced, physically attractive, and behaves decently in the school and out-of-school environment; whereas it is enormously difficult to love a marginalized and less-noticed child. Love children that lag behind academically, misbehave, and tend to break norms of teacher-student interaction. Love children that have alternative health and children from single-parent families. Love those who are less noticed and less loved among their peers.

If you love each child as your own offspring, not a single economic crisis or rigid educational reform will be able to shatter your pedagogical attitude to children and to your profession. Take responsibility for the academic achievement and behavior of every pupil in the same manner as an educator-parent cares for his own child's academic progress and discipline.

Ending this section, I will gladly repeat some significant points. The teaching profession differs from other human occupations and requires specific approaches. *It is the unloved or less loved learners that teachers have to love most.* It may be a boring job but loving the unloved is our moral and, I should say, divine duty and obligation. We, educators, parents, community members, and just adults, must reach out to the most ignored, most unseen, and most forgotten children. However one calls them, they are the overlooked victims of our reasoning civilization. Finding them, helping them, and putting them right is like finding our "lost sheep" and "lost sons." Even if there is only one misbehaving kid in class, our goal is to find and "heal" him, and I am sure that the celebration and rejoice will be great.

It so happens that not only do some children remain unseen in the teaching process and in society, but the whole foundation of schooling often remains wrongly interpreted and overlooked. I give possible reasons for this misinterpretation in the next section.

*Chapter 9*

# NEGLECT OF STRONG BASIC EDUCATION

*Amongst all things, knowledge is truly the best thing;
from its not being liable ever to be stolen, from its not
being purchasable, and from its being imperishable.*
Hindu proverb

*Their knowledge being complete, their thoughts
were sincere.*
Confucian saying

What is a major threat challenging humanity in contemporary epoch? To this question, I have a lucid answer, an answer I have been thinking of, and tortured by, since my graduation from the university: A major and gradually creeping threat to the whole of humanity is the negligence of a strong and lasting secondary education.

## IS LIFE-LONG EDUCATION A PANACEA?

The thesis supporting the idea of solid secondary education has been almost forgotten mostly under pretence of life-long education. Is there anybody among the civilized earthlings who is against life-long education? It seems that nobody is. Life-long education is a good idea, but its effective strategies and goals should be based on a *prior solid education*. For most people worldwide, this prior education equates with secondary education.

Educators are professional workers who, at one time, graduated from a college or university after they had received their secondary education. So did engineers, bankers, journalists, architects, and physicians. But a sizable part of school graduates have no access to further education. Some join the workforce; others, especially young women, stay at home and raise their kids or work part-time; still others are just unable to find a job. It is for those joining the workforce, for housewives, and for those being unable to continue their school education that our assumption about the necessity of a solid secondary education is particularly *relevant and true*.

## AN AMAZING DISAPPOINTMENT

For years I have been interacting with a wide range of high school students from different cultures. I was amazed and disappointed to find out that some of the graduates did not know elementary things. I remember an eleventh-grader from Las Vegas who did not know who John Wayne was; a tenth-grader from Miami who had no idea where the state of Washington was located and who had opened the Americas for the Europeans; an eleventh-grader from Moscow who failed to show the capital of China on the map; a graduate student from Holland who had no idea about the Roman Empire; another graduate from Holland who was not able to remember the longest river on earth; and a graduate student from Scotland who did not know the author of *Treasure Island*.

My hair stood on end when a school graduate in Russia was not able to show on a map where Saint-Petersburg, Russia's second largest city, was located. I was utterly discouraged when a pre-service student of mine mixed up the names of the Russian President and Prime Minister. Equally, I was saddened to learn that a student of mine studying by correspondence (a working teacher!) had no idea who Mark Twain was. With a sad feeling in my heart did I come to learn that most of the graduate students, both at school and university levels, do not possess sufficient knowledge of the facts without which a normal interaction in a normal human society becomes difficult and embarrassing.

How will an average contemporary graduate be able to critically analyze national and international situations and come to adequate decisions if he or she receives a poor secondary education? How can the graduates of U.S. high schools competently function in the surrounding world if they do not know simple things such as:

- the authors of the Declaration of Independence;
- the mechanism of the functioning of the U.S. government with its executive, legislative, and judicial branches;
- the name of the U.S. president who was elected for a fourth term;
- the authors of *Huckleberry Finn, War and Peace,* and *Robinson Crusoe;*
- the capitals of Canada, Turkey, and Brazil;
- and the location of the Nile, Danube and Volga rivers?

How will graduates of Canadian high schools be prepared to effectively interact on the national and international level, if they do not know that Canada is the second largest country in the world, that it is considered the best country in the world in which to live, that it ranks among the world's leaders in per capita spending on public education, and that Bryan Adams is a Canadian musician?

How will school graduates in Brazil be able to identify themselves in their home country and abroad if they do not know that the Amazon Rainforest has the greatest biological diversity in the world, that Rio de Janeiro is the most visited city in the southern hemisphere, and that Brazil is the largest Lusophone or Portuguese-speaking nation-state?

Will it be possible for school graduates from India to properly find themselves in this turbulent world if they are not knowledgeable about Bollywood in Mumbai as being one of the largest centers of film production in the world, Sanskrit as being closely related to the ancient history and culture of India, and the Taj Mahal as being included as one of the New Seven Wonders of the World?

Should every youth carry a laptop to quickly dive into the Internet to fish out a required data or information? I do not think that this is a reliable way out of this situation. It is obviously clear that globalizational processes, the ever-emerging technological innovations, and scientific advancements may quickly outdate any piece of recent knowledge. Yesterday's scientific decisions may become outdated today. We should reassess and refresh facts, knowledge, and information as their significance changes with a changing society.

However, there exist such phenomena and things in our materialistic and spiritual world that *stay intact* for years, centuries and, even eons. For instance, Buddhism was founded in India by Siddhartha Gautama (563-483 B.C.); Christianity emerged in the 1st century; the telephone was invented in 1876; Alexander Fleming discovered penicillin in 1928; and World War II ended in 1945. Native Americans have for centuries lived on the territory of contemporary United States and the Portuguese explorer Ferdinand Magellan was first to sail from the Atlantic Ocean into the Pacific Ocean in 1519-1522. It is impossible to change these historical facts and dates!

# NEGATIVE FACTORS

Factors hindering the process of developing a strong knowledge base, fundamental skills, and basic humanitarian values are the following:

*A Superficial Understanding of the Essence of Secondary Education.* Many people take secondary education as being just one and small step towards further professional and life-long education and governments and educational structures as waiting for and being ready to receive all the schools graduates with stretched arms in order to continually provide all of them with further education and nurturing. In real life things stand otherwise. Tens of millions school graduates across the globe have to spend the rest of their lives without touching a good book except for watching a few TV channels, looking through some newspapers now and then, and hearing some bits of news from a neighbor.

*Predominant Orientation on Decision-Making and Social Action Skills.* It is in the western hemisphere that education policy makers and educators themselves began shattering and destroying the foundations of classic and strong education by "crying out loud" about the benefits of decision-making and critical-thinking skills. I do not want to say that such abilities are not needed in educating the young. Such abilities are and must be an invaluable component of any school and university program. The overall distress over it is that the voices have long been echoing in favor of developing *these and only these* types of skills, to the detriment of ensuring students' strong and high-quality knowledge base and humanistic values and virtues. We have begun ignoring one essential prerequisite: Developing decision-making, problem-solving, and social-action skills requires that students possess a strong body of knowledge, well-known historical facts, and important information.

## LACK OF CORRECT REVISION

A proverb says, "Repetition is the mother of learning." Many teachers and education policy makers fall into the trap of a false assumption by considering that a piece of knowledge once learned can remain for good in a child's long-term memory. Most newly learned material is known to be forgotten within twenty-four hours or so. Then, how can we hope that children will acquire a strong knowledge base if we, being aware of the forgetful nature of the human brain, rigidly believe in the motto "Once heard, forever learned?"

## LINEAR FORMS OF REVISION

Another ineffective practice is the linear or step-by-step forms of revision when, after each unit, educators assess only the most recently acquired knowledge. For example, in the month of October they may test the material learned in September, in November, the material acquired in October and so forth. Can a teacher be confident that the material having learned in September will have been kept in memory sufficiently well by the month of May of the same academic year?

## WEAK CLASSROOM MANAGEMENT

Inadequate classroom control and poor discipline hamper a wide range of academic issues including students' retention and learning abilities. When educators experience constant problems with managing children's behavior, less time is left for developing a strong knowledge base, humanitarian attitudes, and essential skills. Likewise, less time is left for developing their clarified cultural, national, and global identifications.

## PREDOMINANT ORIENTATION ON STANDARDIZED TESTING

Standardized or external tests have both positive and negative influence on students' learning abilities. They provide an accurate comparison across classes, schools or even countries and decrease the subjective influence of teachers on assessment processes. At the same time standardized testing requires that students achieve specific scores, thus forcing teachers to end up "teaching to the test." Such tests hinder the development of students' logical thinking and place a great amount of stress both on learners and teachers. Most important, such tests do not allow educators to effectively and *judiciously* monitor students' day-to-day knowledge base and skills.

It is important to bear in mind that a strong and high-quality education has nothing to do with an authoritarian approach such as one in which the educator forces students to obey strict rules, neglects their individual cognitive characteristics, and sustains an unbearably strict discipline in class. Strong education requires avoiding nonstop and excessive experimenting that leads to continual stressful situations, but it does not call for rejecting experimenting at all. Strong education requires the educator to create a favorable and democratic order with assumption of high responsibility both for teachers and learners. The teacher becomes responsible for creating a strong foundation of knowledge and providing a quality and lasting education. The children are expected to be accountable for enriching and sustaining their knowledge, skills, and attitudes that will enable them to become more effective in collaborating with people from different backgrounds and become equal members of human society.

Providing a graduate receives a superficial and weak education at school, the following scenario may one day unfold after his graduation. This graduate may blame himself for having been lazy at school and also blame teachers and the school for providing him with an inadequate education. The graduate is likely to criticize and condemn the national educational system and the overall governmental structures for having built such a system of education that had failed to provide all students with a solid and fundamental education. Imagine that this same scenario would occur in the hearts of the "tens of millions of graduates" I mentioned above!? Wouldn't it be a humanitarian catastrophe? Worse, it may well happen so that such a calamity is right now unfolding in the souls of a multitude of people having been deprived of a strong secondary education.

I summarize the questions under analysis with several key principles for educators:

## Seek to Provide Students with a Solid Education

For a great number of school graduates secondary education is the only organized education they may ever be able to afford. Alexander Solzhenitsyn (2002), a Nobel Prize winner, says: "Secondary education should be complete and full so that a person could live his life with a proud head, even without having a higher education. It [education] must be valuable and fundamental" (p. 107). All further education, both formal and non-formal, is virtually based on this foundation and stronghold.

Do not equate strong education with the violation of human rights and strict discipline with an authoritarian approach targeted at forcing children to strictly obey educators' orders and making them learn only what educators ask.

It is time to recollect the Japanese proverb reading that "Education is what is left after everything else has been forgotten." This prudent statement incorporates an in-depth idea that initial (school) education needs to be solid and long-lasting. All this means that it is important for a student to show academic competency on a daily basis; but it is much more important for the student to sustain subsequent knowledge, skills, and attitudes after learning each theme and at the end of each academic year. It is also essential that corresponding social action and critical-thinking skills are firmly grasped by the time the student receives the school certificate.

## Provide Students with Knowledge-Clusters

Whenever possible, present knowledge by clustering it within certain topics or blocks. For instance, the knowledge clustering strategy for American high school students can be realized within the following blocks: the United States as a multicultural nation, the U.S. government, environmental problems, energy resources, water resources, health problems, the natural wonders of the world, art and music, science and technology, noted personalities, computers and related technology, and sports in America. It is easier to remember facts and information and develop students' value system when information, knowledge, and facts are brought together in units. Instrumental in this endeavor is to recommend students to use different almanacs and reference books, which contain important information and statistical material on many essential topics.

## Rescue Students from Getting Lost in the Labyrinths of Sources

Monitor the ways how students search for information in various digital and traditional, textual sources. In this information-packed and turbulent age, it may sound a little bit conservative, but among other possible sources, there should be at least one good textbook on each subject area, the content of which children must know well. Each textbook is expected to be complied by a team of knowledgeable experts on the subject area. Knowledge continually changes and becomes outdated, and no textbook can contain material that will last for decades. Therefore, this "golden" textbook should be updated as frequently as possible. At least, each year a new enrolment of children should be expected to start a new academic year with an updated edition.

Select as the main source the most suitable textbook among the ones recommended by the curriculum. Also, select additional and supplementary sources. It is quite obvious that learners are unable to simultaneously and productively use a number of textbooks as the main source of information and knowledge in learning each discipline.

## Develop Firm Skills

In addition to strong knowledge, promote firm skills required by the curriculum and by the moral, civic, and humanitarian demands. By the notion of firm, I mean automatic skills, "easily downloadable" from the memory reservoirs when needed.

Starting from early childhood, we must make habitual and automatic the maximum number of useful actions in children, and, at the same time, prevent harmful habit and skills from taking root and becoming automatic. In other words, the more useful actions of children are made automatic (to the extent when these actions do not require any extra effort in their performance), the more room will be left in their intellectual and cognitive reservoirs for developing their highest spiritual and other important capabilities (Vygotsky, 1991).

## Organize a Proper Revision

One of the prerequisites of making knowledge strong and long-lasting is a continual and purposeful revision by adding subsequent novel knowledge to previously learned material. When an educator presents information to students, it goes to the working memory and may fade away very soon. To store the information in the long-term memory, an intensive and repetitive practice is needed.

Do not forget the proverb: "Repetition is the mother of learning." During a successive lesson, apart from the planned revision lessons and planned oral, written, or computer-based tests, try to undertake a quick, two-to-three-minute revision of recently taught material. In another lesson, revise a wider scope of the past material. A continual revision yields fruitful results. This simple system, based on both conscious and subconscious techniques of revision, helps students retain the material stronger. When the goals are set to retain the material thoroughly, it is necessary to frequently use both external tests and non-test strategies such as performance assessment, small group discussion, brainstorming, and question-response techniques.

## Help Children Train Their Memories

A human being possesses a fantastic and amazing ability to keep information and knowledge in memory. In the learning process, students have greater possibilities to regularly increase their abilities to receive, store, retain and productively use information, knowledge, and facts. However, teachers and parents should help children to *additionally ameliorate* their memory capacities.

An individual's memory works more actively and effectively when directed by personal motives and positive emotions and impulses. The quality of acquiring and retaining information is also dependent on how intensely a child can concentrate on the target material. Children's attention, especially at pre-school and elementary school levels, tends to be distractible. To remember something well, as Vygotsky assumed, a learner is recommended to "collect the organism into one dot." In other words, the learner must *strongly focus attention on a particular task* and keep it there.

Help students understand that memory is an invaluable thing when it comes to cognitive activity. Teach your students to train their memories by using effective methods for reinforcing their memory capacities. An effective technique for strengthening students' memory is regular repetition of the past material by consciously linking it with new items of information and knowledge. Also, recommend your students to read a good book on memory and memory training.

## Create a Favorable Classroom Environment

An important premise for providing students with a strong education is based on creating a favorable and productive learning environment so as to encourage their academic and personality growth. In building a pedagogically and psychological favorable atmosphere, much depends on managing the class as a whole body while attending to each individual separately. Moreover, students should have a clear understanding of the fact that not only educators but also *they, themselves,* are accountable and responsible for their academic progress.

As was underlined in a previous chapter, there is also a close relationship between teaching/learning and classroom control. The more educators involve learners in cognitive activity, the fewer difficulties arise with classroom management; conversely, the more able educators are in organizing the class and handling discipline, the easier the process of teaching and learning becomes. Consequently, the process of gaining a solid and strong education is facilitated.

The school is a primary socio-educational cell for a child until he or she graduates from it, and the cohort of educators a child deals with are pedagogical pastors. An outstanding role is assigned to the elementary teacher who should build the primary foundation, an unbreakable rock upon which other educators in subsequent years will contribute blocks of knowledge, skills, and values.

A weak secondary education may be likened to a house built on sand. When rains fall and winds blow, the weak foundation will fall with a "great crash." A solid and strong education is like a house erected on the rock, i.e. on a strong basis. No "rains," "streams" or "winds" will be able to crash such a foundation and stronghold.

I do not reject the ideas of life-long and distance education, which are in fact, one of the main goals of combating illiteracy on the global scale. These ideas are mostly targeted to include the excluded and reach the rejected, those who have already been educationally and intellectually marginalized. The idea of a strong secondary education is a doctrine directed at those who are *now* in school and at those who will step onto the school threshold *tomorrow.* It is secondary education that should become a solid and strong foundation for further professional education, and undoubtedly, for life-long education.

In striving to provide learners with strong education, educators and parents have to cope with a problem sweeping all over the global educational space. What sort of problem is it and how should we solve it? To begin with, let us open the next page.

# Chapter 10

# ENSLAVEMENT BY THE VIRTUAL REALITY

> *Computers are magnificent tools for the realization of our dreams,*
> *but no machine can replace the human spark of spirit, compassion,*
> *love, and understanding.*
> Louis Gerstner

> *Many people are awaiting Virtual Reality,*
> *I'm awaiting virtuous reality.*
> Eli Khamarov

Owing to ultramodern communication technologies, our contemporary era is witnessing an unprecedented expansion and dissemination of information and knowledge. The notions of *cyberspace, digital space (world),* and *digital technology* have emerged and spread worldwide. Cyberspace is a term describing anything related to human communication or exchange of ideas or to any other possible activity in the global network. Computers and other digital technologies are changing the ways we perform our professional responsibilities, communicate with the outer world, spend money and pay the bills, buy and sell things, and entertain ourselves. Such technologies may partly or fully influence a human being's personal fame or career advancement or, conversely, maximize his immoral downfall or career loss. By creating innovative and super modern information and communication technologies, humanity is altering and reorganizing the space-time continuum. Modern technologies have become indispensable components of the educational process and made us think differently about teaching and learning. Students get to knowledge, data, and information escaping textbooks and teacher's knowledge arsenal.

My assumption is that the virtual or artificial reality has existed ever since human beings began their creative activity, when they started erecting statues of art, writing poems and novels, and opening the laws of physics and chemistry. First, it was a "young," non-technological reality. This reality did exist in the collective consciousness of people, especially in the minds of noted personalities who were themselves creating this reality. For example, to such people belonged Leonardo da Vinci, Peter the Great, George Washington, and Mother Teresa. In due time, this reality incorporated the literary personages such as Camelot, Tom Sawyer, Robinson Crusoe, D'Artanyan, and Count of Monte Cristo; the paintings such as *Mona Liza, Sistine Madonna,* and *Gernica;* and the man-made monuments such as the Great Wall of China and the Eiffel Tower. The virtual reality humanity is currently shaping and plunged into is another but, inevitably, decisive step forward.

## NATURE AND NURTURE

Some psychologists and educators claim that two huge variables influence child development—nature referring to an individual's biological inheritance and nurture dealing with his or her environmental experiences. Others maintain that child rearing processes are under the influence of pedagogical, environmental, and hereditary factors. Still others, using simplified terminology, support the idea that child development is influenced by family, school, and society. It is easy to conclude that all three groups presuppose the same thing: Child development is under the continual influence of both inner (hereditary) and outer (pedagogical, societal and parental) factors.

Today, in addition to the objective reality surrounding us, there has come into being another entity—the virtual reality. Thus, I venture to acknowledge that the chain of factors drawing forth child development incorporates five intertwined links or factors such as hereditary, parental (factors pertaining to the process of upbringing in the family circle), pedagogical (factors referring to formal education), societal (factors lying outside school and family), and virtual.

# VIRTUAL REALITY

Virtual realty is an artificial world whose time has come. An average school and college student spends a considerable portion of his conscious life in this reality. In the years to come, the possibilities of the virtual world of facts, information, and entertainment will grow exponentially. I admit that there exist two clear-cut realities we live in: The objective reality that surrounds us and that we perceive by seeing, hearing, touching, and smelling, and a virtual reality that exists somewhere "within" the digital technology.

Contemporary young people are being bombarded with information and messages in their email boxes. After lesson sessions, they are almost continually attached to some information-generating device—the Internet, mobile phone, iPad, Black-Berry, iPhone. Among other small stuff that girls carry in their bags and boys in their pockets are two indispensable items—a cell phone and a flash drive. The cell phone has become a super important medium for socializing, and some children often avoid interaction with peers who do not have such phones.

Other possibilities being equal, there is nothing wrong in children's using the Internet, cell phones, TV channels and other technologies to access, digest, and use the knowledge and information embedded within these devices. The virtual reality is a place where the whole world—with its labyrinths of interaction and with the newly emerging news and facts—is being assembled. The world has become small, approaches us, and is knocking at our doors through digital media.

The main container of the virtual world, the Internet, is forcing out DVDs, CVs, land line telephones, libraries, museums and what not! The cell phone tries not to lag behind! Partly replacing television, the Internet has become an invaluable asset in almost all man-made public places and institutions—kindergartens; schools; colleges and universities; different offices; libraries; shopping centers; restaurants, hotels, and resorts; tea and coffee houses; railway stations, river ports, seaports, and airports; and hospitals and clinics.

Super-technologies have brought about new behaviors and new ways of learning. Students have replaced much of their factual learning by compressing it into a flash drive. Textbook material has been replaced with the information from the Internet. Learners tend to voluntarily seek out expertise beyond the classroom and school.

## THE POSITIVE SIDES OF DIGITAL TECHNOLOGIES

The advantageous sides of television, computers, and related digital technologies are numerous and enormous in scope. Among other inventions, the most colossal potential is embedded in the Internet. It is continuously being enriched and expanded from within. Most of the information and data are being updated regularly. When used judiciously, the Internet (1) enhances children's imagination and creativity; (2) helps find practically any information by writing a suitable keyword on the screen and clicking the mouse; (3) enhances their knowledge base on historical and current events, on creative biographies and achievements of world-famous personalities whose personal lives and contributions to humanity are worth considering or, maybe, worth following as a model; (4) promotes the acquisition of knowledge about different cultures and ethnic groups, thus fostering children's multicultural and global competency; (5) provides messages promoting citizenship and responsible actions and prosocial behavior; (6) helps combine the textual material with pictorial images, which accelerates comprehension and understanding of a given theme; (7) and helps build virtual groups of people (scientists, educators, musicians and so forth) whose mutual interests may influence human society.

## THE NEGATIVE SIDES OF DIGITIZATION

On the other hand, digital technologies have, in the last few decades, begun to disappoint people and especially parents, educators, and the main "trouble-makers"--youngsters. It appears that progress is a tricky thing and has a precarious side. Leo Tolstoy (1989), a writer, pedagogue, and connoisseur of human soul, noticed that "progress in one side [of life] is always ransomed by a regression in some other side of human life" (p. 255). With reference to the influx of digital technology, his prophetic assumption has come true with a fantastic exactness.

What are the detrimental sides of Internet use? What harm does it bring to children of school and college age? Under the conditions of ill-considered and obsessive use, the Internet:

- takes time away from productive and health enhancing activities;
- hinders the academic progress of students, because it impairs the ability to attend to cognitive assignments recommended by the curriculum;
- brings children to social isolation;
- may convey and perpetuate stereotypes about particular ethnic, cultural, religious, and gender groups;
- breeds cognitive passivity because the user gets into the habit of following the directions of both complicated and trifling answers. There were frequent occasions when my students applied to their cell phone Internet any time there was a need of even a minor mathematical or other logical and mental manipulation;
- reduces the role of students' live speech;
- hinders creative and logical thinking. Internet use makes a person's thinking adjust to certain rules, models, and formal logical structures and perform operations that have only one outcome;
- influences young people's ways of thinking. The more they get involved in viewing Internet sites and television programs, the more their minds are shaped by the messages that these realities present;
- unintentionally depicts various advertisements most of which boost new goods and products (the ones people are often loath to buy) and often promotes youngsters' materialistic and consumer orientations;
- leads to an addiction when a user obsessively exploits the Internet. Among other age groups, children, teenagers, and young adults are more likely to get addicted by the Internet.

## INTERNET ADDICTION

This term emerged somewhere in the 1980s-1990s and currently is widely used because there is a strong evidence that such an addiction exists. The symptoms are comparable to other compulsive disorders such as gambling, using narcotics and alcohol, watching television, and overeating. Addiction is a dependence on habit which begins to dominate an individual's life. As a result, the individual's behavior becomes obsessive and enslaved by a given "favorite activity."

Internet addiction often masks other problems such as social anxiety, low self-esteem, loneliness, depression, school or work difficulties, and marital problems. Of all addictions, Internet addiction is not the worst, but it is a unique dependence because children do not have to hide this habit like drug or alcohol addicts do. Internet addicts may use the screen in all possible places, both secluded and public. One of the main drivers of Internet addiction among children and adolescents are game and cybersex sites.

# GAME ADDICTION

As medical and other specialists ascertain, the consequences of gaming addiction include:

- incapability of regulating and planning time. Video game use becomes more important for children than fulfilling the assignment required by the curriculum. Children may play for hours forgetting all that surrounds them;
- sleep-related disorders such as parasomnia (nightmares, night terrors), insomnia, and sleep apnea (abnormal pauses in breathing or instances of abnormally low breathing);
- back pains owing to sitting in the same position for hours on end;
- neglect of personal hygiene. Taking care of one's body, hair, and teeth becomes less of a priority;
- eating disorders. Irregularities with eating bring another trouble to young people obsessed with games. They either loose weight or, contrarily, gain it. In other cases, unhealthy and unbalanced meals may lead to more serious physical disorders;
- carpal tunnel syndrome. It occurs as a tingling in three fingers (thumb, index finger, and middle finger) accompanied by wrist pain. This syndrome occurs when the carpal tunnel (the area of the wrist housing the main nerve and tendons) becomes swollen and irritated.

Most games have an end, but, in the multiplayer, there are numerous variations, therefore children can play and reenter endlessly. The games found on mobile phones are also addictive and they can be played right in front of the teacher's nose.

An addiction to games has social consequences. When a young person is obsessed by video games, his or her real world tends to disappear into a cyberworld. To me, it seems like this cyberworld swallows the realistic human world or reality like a black hole can swallow any cosmic objects, even stellar systems and galaxies. Gaming takes priority above other important things and activities. Plunged into the labyrinths of artificial reality and being fully dependent on it, the users forget about the surrounded reality and personal relationships. Games and their content become central topics of their communication with peers and adults. A long-lasting game addiction hinders effective socialization and the maintenance of healthy relationships in school premises and beyond.

## VIDEO AND INTERNET SEX ADDICTION

An addiction of children and teenagers to viewing erotic and pornographic photos and movies is one of the serious problems related to computer and video use. Such content is at the closest reach of young people of any age, including even pre-school kids. Clinicians studying sex addiction have noticed that the compulsive viewing of pornography has led to the issues necessitating treatment (Pollets, 2008).

Early exposure to pornographic and erotic scenes provides the worst example of an "involuntary and hidden sexual education." I use the word *involuntary* because sexual scenes can emerge on the Internet screen quite of a sudden, even without a user's will to watch them. By *hidden* I mean a non-formal sexual education and the most hazardous side of it when it shatters and destroys children's psychic systems, deprives them of their childhood and adolescence, and makes them slaves of their emotions and desires. The phenomenon of porn addiction has been generating an increased concern since children began using the Internet.

Specialists and evidence indicate that porn addiction escalates the desire to view more material with sexual content, which, in turn, quickly undermines the addicts' psychological and emotional state. This syndrome of progressing addiction to video porn takes childhood away from a child and teenhood from a teenager and molds them into "young adults" who become prematurely knowledgeable about all secrets of adult life. It engenders sleep problems that may be similar to the ones experienced by game addicts but complemented by dreaming of various erotic and sexually oriented scenes and scenes of violence. All this negatively impacts children's and adolescents' nervous systems.

A craving for porn viewing tempts young ones to resort to masturbation or sexual stimulation of genitals and erotic zones to experience sexual pleasure or orgasm. An individual may masturbate in the process of viewing erotic or porn scenes or immediately after watching them. In doing so, there is a threat of becoming a compulsive lover of masturbation. Being dependent on masturbation, in turn, makes the individual resort to porn viewing in order to satisfy his or her sexual drive. One can only imagine what nervous and emotional damage this exclusive and secluded cycle brings to young ones. In the case when compulsive masturbation is not driven by an addiction to viewing porn, it may be a sign of some other emotional problem.

Porn addiction develops early incentives and abnormal drives to sexual activity with opposite-sex and same-sex peers. The addict openly views the scenes of immorality with people involved in an unprotected lovemaking with casual partners, even strangers. Sooner or later, cybersex addiction may motivate the youngster to incline to sexual activity a partner and imitate the ways of sexual behavior and abnormal sex depicted in erotic and pornographic photos and movies.

An excessive use of erotic and pornographic sites may ignite a desire to "strengthen" one's sexual drives by consuming alcoholic beverages, strong coffee, smoking, and by using drugs. Like compulsive masturbation, regular alcohol and drug use ignited by intensive viewing of pornography sites can itself continually "return" a boy or a girl to viewing erotic and sexual sites. In this case, too, we deal with the "notorious" exclusive and secluded cycle. Finding a way out of this vicious cycle may cost tremendous effort and treatment. Porn dependency may stimulate and encourage youngsters to early sexual activity with multiple partners, which may correspondingly instigate the spread of sexually transmitted diseases and increase the incidence of teen pregnancy.

The above-presented discussion thus far leads to several implications for school district authorities and school administrators.

## Measures for Higher Authorities

Dismissing children, adolescents, and young adults completely from computer use is virtually impossible and unwise, which means that we may be thrown back in time for decades. Who wants to replace a computer with a typewriter? Transforming all the efforts of educating the young generation into the rails of digital technology, under the pretence that future belongs to technology use, is equally imprudent. The virtual reality is a subtle, but shaky, risky, and dangerous phenomenon with thousands of pluses and millions of minuses.

However, it becomes important for the holders of private and commercial Web sites to make erotic and pornographic pictures and movies unavailable for pre-school, elementary, and secondary school children. Second, it is necessary to equip school, college, and university computers with modernized Internet filters that can block the visual depictions spoiling the minors' moral, psychological, and physiological conditions.

Blocking pornography sites and monitoring students' activities in virtual reality should not be considered as the violation of human rights and freedom. As we know, freedom borders with responsibility. When dealing with these matters, there should be a definite authoritarian pressure on users on the part of adults. The people who had experienced such a pressure in their younger years will be enormously grateful to those who had protected them from the excessive influence of the digital reality.

What can educators do to prevent students from becoming enslaved by the virtual world? I offer the following suggestions:

## Supervise Children's Use of Computers and Related Technology

Monitor and supervise the ways your children use computers in the school premises, because the cases of addiction to computers and other digital technology are on the rise and represent an ever-growing concern of parents, educators, and public at large. When there are signs of a learner's becoming dependent on Internet use, work in close contact with parents, the school personnel, and, if needed, with specialists who can clear up the situation and recommend required measures.

## Beware of Hackers

Ensure students' and parents' understanding of the fact that any user of the Internet is under constant threat of hackers who illegally connect and use other people's information and email addresses for blackmailing and money laundering. Hackers exploit the weaknesses of the digital system or people's incautious use of computers and email service. Children should not frivolously contact any one and let strangers know their passwords. They also should be cautious to all sorts of junk mail.

## Work with Parents

Steer parents to guide their children's use of digital technology. If any symptoms that a child has started obsessively using the Internet arise, discuss this problem and try to solve it by common efforts. Encourage family members to become active participants in teaching their children how to rationally use digital technology. Parents rarely watch educational and other useful TV programs with their children, and they infrequently discuss the content and problems transmitted in them, not to mention the Internet sites.

I am also a parent and take it as a great omission that I had rarely watched and commented educational and other programs with my son Edward in his middle and late childhood. Feeling ashamed and sorry about my previous negligence, I began to monitor his use of the Internet in his adolescent years. My "post-repentance initiatives" have borne fruit.

Conduct subsequent work with parents and extended family members about harm that viewing pornographic and related sites bring to child and adolescent development. Parents must be alert to what sites their children are interested in. Monitor students' online activities, at least through the school computer system.

We live in an informational and digital epoch. Humanity is moving forward. We have not yet fully become conscious about how quickly computers and mobile phones have colonized our minds. In reasonable proportions and with due precaution, using digital technologies makes great breakthroughs in cognizing the objective reality and helps young people and adults in their professional activity and everyday lives. In reasonable amounts, even video games can be helpful for children's development.

## Encourage but not Deify

While encouraging pupils to use technology, do not deify computers, television and related technology as the easiest and the sole reliable means of gaining knowledge and information. To gain knowledge, students should use, in addition to mandatory textbooks, all the non-technological sources such as various books, reference literature, magazines, journals, and newspapers. Teach them how to find and use library sources. Nudge your students into visiting museums, exhibitions, book fairs, and festive events, where they can gain a variety of useful and interesting information and facts. Bring and encourage them to read geographic, economic and other maps ranging from that of your district to those of your country and the world. In my professional practice I often discover that some in-service and pre-service teachers are not very knowledgeable about the geographical location of some continents, oceans, and major countries that play an important role in the vortex of globalization and international events.

## Be Alert to Students' Gaming and Pornography Addiction

When a student is obsessively dependent on video games or porno sites, the symptoms of addiction are similar to those I provided previously. An addiction to games usually manifests itself more or less openly. Children may play in the presence of teachers, parents and other people in any place possible: at home, in school premises, in public places and in open areas such as yards, gardens, and parks. As for the addiction to pornography sites, this type of obsession unfolds as a hidden process. In dealing with gaming and pornography addiction, like in many other cases of educating children, a *close contact with other teachers, parents and licensed specialists is needed.* If you follow this golden rule, it will be easier to discover the maladaptive behavior and appropriately discipline and educate the young person caught in the addiction.

## Recognize Computer (Internet) Addiction Symptoms

Previously I enumerated some of the consequences of Internet addiction. In this paragraph I briefly return to them. The consequences include (1) withdrawing from health-enhancing and other pleasurable activities; (2) neglecting friends, family, and, often, all human society; (3) problems in academic performance; (4) being dishonest with others about time spent on computer use; (5) compulsive and aggressive behavior; (6) feelings of guilt, emptiness, and depression; and (7) physical problems such as backaches, headaches, weight gain or loss, and carpal tunnel syndrome. When noticing these signs in your students or if parents or other people complain to you that someone in your class or school is under an abnormal influence of digital technologies and some of these symptoms manifest themselves openly, immediately undertake necessary measures.

## Enforce Preventive Measures

If the addiction is still in the early stages, take preventive measures. Learn more about the phenomenon of computer addiction and how to cope with it. Explain to students and their parents the harm that such addiction brings to young people. It is better to prevent a problem than to courageously rush to solving it when the problem has gone too far.

Discuss each new case with your colleagues and administration and insert corresponding measures to control the school Internet system against students' viewing pornographic, erotic, and other immoral content. The overuse of cell phones has also become a problem invoking concern. It seems that children and adolescents do not part from them since the early hours of the morning till the time they go to bed. I think there should be a law prohibiting students from bringing cell phones to school. If this does not work, ask them to keep them switched off during the lessons and extracurricular activities.

## Replace Addiction with Other Activities

With a persuasion from parents, try to put new ideas on children's minds or replace their obsessive involvement in the Internet with other entertainments and activities. Instead of being inordinately involved in computer use, children may go in for sports, join a club, participate in a church youth group, go hiking or on a family picnic, go outside for a walk with a pet, read an interesting book and discuss its content with peers or parents, and volunteer to participate in some benevolent and charitable project. A girl or a boy may simply spend more time preparing home assignments. Ask parents to limit the amount of time on online work for their children. To beat down the degree of gaming addiction and cut the amount of time their children spend on this enterprise, parents may help their kids choose traditional games and designate special hours to use them.

Digital and other technologies will unlikely "leave" the sphere of education, nor will they disappear in economy, banking, and statistics. Instead, technology will be constantly innovated. I myself remember all major steps of the development of digital technologies, from simple calculators and large-size computers in the 1980s to the personal computers with flash drives in the 2010s. Probably, in the near future, people will be using some sort of minute crystal chips capable of possessing a fantastically great amount of information.

One can only imagine a chip containing all the knowledge and information of the Library of Congress! Another step may be even more crucial when humans will possibly learn to transmit their thoughts to any distant place on earth and materialize them into solid, material forms or when they will be able to read, on a distance, other people's thoughts!

Meanwhile the lives of children and adolescents become increasingly involved in virtual maze. Will educators, parents, and governmental structures be able to cope wisely with this problem? Used wisely, constructively, and moderately, the virtual reality affords a colossal potential for positively effecting children's cognitive activity and developing their global competency and literacy. If used witlessly and senselessly, it contains endless possibilities to swallow children's time, energy, and mind and spoil their lives.

Man is penetrating into the virtual world by continually widening and deepening it. Man is creating this hidden world. What is more dangerous is that this reality, this world of signs, numbers, and information has begun to colonize children's and teenagers' minds and enslave them.

The virtual reality is saluting, parading, and devouring the young and the adult across continents and oceans. While this reality rests on its laurels, educators and students have started forgetting the classics of education who were pioneers in blazing pedagogical trails. The ensuing chapter is specially crafted to bring to mind the pedagogical legacies of five eminent educators.

# Chapter 11

# SHOULD YOUNG EDUCATORS
# FORGET CLASSICS?

*What is above is like what is below,*
*and what has been is like what will be.*
Hermes Trismegistus

*Children's games, sufferings, parents' punishments,*
*books, labor, learning, both forced and free,*
*the arts, science, life--all educate.*
Leo Tolstoy

Some of the young generation of teachers, teacher educators, and students have only a hazy idea of the classics in education. Moreover, some of them have unforgivably forgotten renowned educational thinkers who laid the foundation of our pedagogical science.

Educators are known to rarely create "pleasantly-looking things" such as paintings or frescoes, which could be accessible to the curious audiences. If educators write books and articles, they tend to appeal predominately to people of their own circle and, perhaps, to parents of students. For people from other professions, pedagogical literature may contain "uninteresting material," which may be difficult for understanding at first approach and which may require a considerable effort to digest its content. Obviously, educators can design effective teaching methods; but it is often difficult to implement them in mass practice. If they teach and educate children and adolescents, no one exactly knows what types of personalities these adolescents may become in the future.

In other words, educators are likely to be unseen workers, and the outcomes of their occupation can not be always duly noticed and evaluated both by their colleagues and by people from other walks of life. The goal of this section is an attempt to fill this unseen niche by additionally reminding the reader of the pedagogical legacy of at least five celebrated educators and thinkers.

These five acclaimed personalities are John Amos Comenius, Leo Tolstoy, John Dewey, Maria Montessori, and Lev Vygotsky.

## JOHN AMOS COMENIUS

Comenius (Komenský) was born on March 28, 1592, in Nivnice, Czech Republic. While attending the Latin school in Přerov, Moravia, he consciously came to understand all the drawbacks of the teaching methods practiced at this institution. Later he called his school years as the "lost time." In 1628, together with the Brethren, Comenius had to leave Bohemia for Leszno, Poland, where he created the majority of his pedagogical works that received a worldwide recognition. He had to live and work in many countries of Europe, including England, Sweden, Hungary, and Holland. In 1650 he set up a pansophic school in Hungary. The last fourteen years of his life he resided in Amsterdam, where he died on November 15, 1670 (Piskunov, 2005; "Comenius," 2009).

His pedagogical legacy is saturated with the *idea of pansophy*--a universal system of human knowledge and wisdom among all individuals and nations. The underlying assumption of this system rests on the premise that any growing individual is required to be a reasonable being, capable of investigating and understanding the essence of everything in the world. Such human beings should (1) use surrounding things properly for their own betterment as well as for public benefit, and (2) monitor their inner and outer intentions.

Ensuing from the pansophic theory was Comenius' idea of a *nature-conformable education*. Basing on the principle of the unity of the laws of nature and education, he recommended keeping to the four stages of teaching: the first stage--independent observation; the second-- practical implementation; the third--the use of the acquired knowledge, skills, and habits in novel situations; and the fourth stage--the ability to independently interpret the results of cognitive activity.

Comenius' educational insights and recommendations were expressed in his epoch-making book *Didactica Magna* (Great Didactics). Taking as a basis the fundamentals of the nature-conformable education, he formulated the following generalized strategy: In teaching, students should first see and observe objects; and it is only after this stage of cognition that they may embark on a discussion of the corresponding objects. He formulated this assumption in his "golden rule" (cited in Piskunov, 2005): "Whatever possible, it is necessary to cognize what is observable--by eyesight, what is heard--by ear, smells--by smelling, what is subject to taste--by tasting, and what is perceived by tactile sensation--by touching. If some objects can be perceived by several senses, let them be immediately grasped by several senses..." (p. 190).

At the same time he recommended using subsidiary means--pictures, drawings, models and so forth--to motivate and enhance children's cognitive abilities.

Comenius devoted himself to combating obsolete and medieval norms in education. He was one of the first pedagogues who quested for and systematized the objective laws of child development. He tried to solve those problems which had gone unanswered in earlier times.

To all the educators of the world and public at large he became known as the *teacher of nations and the father of modern education*. Also, John Comenius can be unmistakably named as the *pioneer of education*. So great and enormous is his contribution into various aspects of education! There are too many firsts in the sphere of education, especially in the science of didactics, which he designed and implemented. In fact, at the core of a considerable number of didactic principles being now used daily in classrooms all over the world lie the fundamental rules worked out by Comenius!

# LEO TOLSTOY

Tolstoy was born on September 9, 1828 at Yasnaya Polyana in Tula Province, Russia. In 1844 he entered Kazan University but, dissatisfied by the standards of education, left it in 1847. In the 1850s Tolstoy started his literary career, and in the 1860s he concretely engaged in the pedagogical activity, which he never stopped. He traveled in Europe seeing places and investigating the issues of pedagogical theory and practice. He visited various educational institutions and participated in classroom work in France, England, and

Germany. In 1862 he married Sonya Behrs, who bore him 13 children and was his devoted secretary. Tolstoy died on November 20, 1910.

Tolstoy's creative activity as a pedagogue is traditionally divided into three periods. During the first period (1859-1862) he obsessively studied pedagogical literature and opened a school for peasants' children at Yasnaya Polyana. He insisted that children of peasants and children of simple origin should receive an education of the same quality as received by children from the elite circles. He believed that all education should be *free and voluntary* and that the "sole method of education is experience, and its only criterion is freedom" (Tolstoy, 1989, p. 70). The school at Yasnaya Poliana appeared to be a unique creative laboratory, the principles of which--*experience and freedom*--became key directives not only in pedagogy but in many other sides of the creative development of man. In 1862 there existed around thirteen rural schools in which Tolstoy's pedagogical techniques and recommendations were being implemented.

In his view, there is no best method in subject area instruction. The best method is the one that the teacher knows best. Each good teacher tends to use his or her method that should only be developed and perfected continually. He wrote: "To become a literate person as quickly as possible, any one person should be taught in an exclusive, individual manner; therefore there should be a special method for each learner" (p. 88).

During the second period (1870-1876) he worked at compiling the ABC-book for children, continued teaching the peasants' children, and, overcoming bureaucratic barriers, succeeded in persuading the local school district authorities to raise the salaries of the teachers working in rural schools. The third period (1880-1910) was marked by his writing a number of manuals and short stories for children. In the 1890s Tolstoy severely criticized the authorities for their incapability to combat the societal ulcers such as corruption, prostitution, alcohol abuse, homicide, superstition, and brutality toward poor people.

What Tolstoy succeeded in the theory and practice of education has made a global impact on advancing and bettering many sides of child development and child-rearing. He is acclaimed as one of the brilliant educational reformers. Experimental sites and schools in Europe and America have taken into account his ideas and profited from his experiential legacy.

His striving to defend the personality of the child, to condemn the authoritarian style of teaching and teacher-student interaction, and to support new pedagogical approaches, his innovative and brave recommendations, and his practical didactic methods were supported and taken up by the progressive educators at the rise of the 20th century and onwards. Tolstoy may be considered as one of the fervent supporters of the global movement of teachers for democratization of teacher-child relationships (Kudriavaya, 1993).

He raised his voice in favor of qualitative education of peasants' children, who are least noticed when the question of education of the growing generation is concerned. He noticed that in villages there were many talented and gifted children who, when approached with proper methods of teaching, might perform wonders.

Count Tolstoy was an original and independent thinker. He could agree or disagree with his interlocutor and be apt in providing his assumptions with pertinent arguments. He has left to the posterity truly exceptional and incomparably wise sayings. For example, he considered the family as an important union between man and woman. His iconic novel *Anna Karenina* opens with the great phrase: "Happy families are all alike, every unhappy family is unhappy in its own way." It might be a hard job to live a long monogamic family-life, but family problems--divorces, family quarrels, singe-parent families, alcohol and drug abuse, and adultery--cannot escape the attention of children and teenagers. These and other parental caprices negatively impact on child development and child socialization.

# JOHN DEWEY

I came to learn about John Dewey when I was a tenth-grader. I accidentally opened a page in an encyclopedia containing his short biography. Without attaching any particular notice to the details, I, however, fixed his name and the fact that he was a celebrated philosopher and educator in my mind. At university and later years, I read a lot of material that had been written by and about him.

He was born on October 20, 1859, at Burlington, Vermont, the United States. After attending public schools, he entered the University of Vermont. In 1884 he was awarded the Ph.D. degree at Johns Hopkins University, after which he worked at the University of Michigan, the University of Chicago, and at Columbia University. After World War I he traveled a lot: lecturing at the Imperial Institute in Japan (1919), teaching at the Chinese universities of Nanking and Peking (1919-21), and visiting Turkey (1924), Mexico (1926), and the Soviet Union (1928). He became a widely known pedagogue and philosopher in America and in the whole world. All his life Dewey remained a prolific writer and published over 300 works. He died on June 1, 1952.

Dewey's original philosophical orientation was called *pragmatism* or instrumentalism, which means that different types of human activity represent instruments developed to solve individual and social problems. The human quest for truth must be based on experience. His endeavors in philosophy were largely centered in education. He concluded that learning arises from the personal experience of a child when he starts solving a problem. The principle *learn by doing* became central in his educational creed. An important objective of the method Dewey proposed was developing the child as a whole being. His concept of learning was far different and much more progressive than the earlier and existing educational traditions, which had failed to meet the requirements of the latest findings in child development and the demands of the changing democratic society.

He insisted that an individual should continually reorganize and rethink past experiences in the light of new ones. For Dewey, ideas and experiences which are not intertwined with the growing experience and knowledge but remain isolated seemed a waste of precious time. This postulation is exactly in consonance with what Lev Vygotsky proposed when addressing the issues of teaching and child-upbringing, which I will further discuss.

Dewey underlined the importance of providing children with problematic situations which promote their reflective thinking. His model for learning included the following steps of cognitive activity: (1) becoming aware of a problem which arises out of present experiences; (2) speculating over and defining the problem; (3) observing the relevant data; (4) formulating the relevant hypothesis; (5) finding a way to solve the problem and predict the results comparing it with similar situations; and (6) testing the proposed hypothesis and objectives (Bim-Bad, 2002).

The great pedagogue and philosopher believed that (1) the *school is a social institution*; (2) any individual attending school is a social being; (3) education is not a preparation for future living but a real process of living; (4) education must be conceived as a constant reconstruction of experience; (5) education represents the fundamental method of social progress; and (6) the teacher does not simply train individuals but forms the proper social life (Dewey, 1897).

John Dewey's educational and humanitarian legacy has been and is making a considerable global impact on the systems of education in many countries. His wise teaching on democracy and its relation to education often come to the minds of contemporary educators and researchers who seek to reform and modernize their professional activity and enrich their research programs. His ideas of experiential learning are implemented in the Eurasian countries, where these ideas are collectively addressed as the project method of learning. This method is currently widely used in Russia's high schools and universities as one of the progressive strategies of cognizing the objective reality. This method is premised on a step-by-step approach, which means that a given student is required, first, to select a topic; second, "enter" and grasp the main essence of it; third, formulate the hypothesis and put forward goals for solving it; fourth, realize the hypothesis; and, fifth, to adequately evaluate the outcomes and data received

## MARIA MONTESSORI

Born in the town of Chiaravalle, Italy, on August 31, 1870, Montessori became the first female physician in Italy upon graduation from a medical school in 1895. In 1904 she ranked as a professor of anthropology at the University of Rome. Later she founded the first *Casa dei Bambini* (Children's House) in the San Lorenzo district in Rome. The method of teaching that Montessori designed and implemented was based on *furthering the self-creating process of the child*. Soon she was heard in the United Stated where she was strongly supported by Alexander Graham Bell, Thomas Edison, and Helen Keller. In 1913 Graham Bell and his wife founded the Montessori Educational Association in Washington.

Because she opposed the Mussolini's policy of fascism, she had to leave Italy in 1934 and continued disseminating her educational approaches in Spain, Great Britain, the Netherlands, India, and Germany. Montessori was nominated for the Nobel Peace Prize three times--in 1949, 1950, and in 1951. She died in Noordwijk, Holland, on May 6, 1952.

Montessori begins the methodology and dialectic substantiation of her educational approach by stating that the child, living alongside the adult, virtually remains alien to the social life and labor activity of the adult. In all adult world, the child seems to be a desruptive outsider intruding on the surrounding people. The personality of the little one remains buried under the prejudices of order and the adults' ways of life. At the same time the child is utterly dependent on the adult, and his or her social rights are not seriously taken into account. Montessori states (cited in Oswald & Schulz-Benesch, 1997):

> The fact that the right of the child has been forgotten and ignored,
> that the child has been mistreated, even destroyed, and that moreover his

worth, power and nature have been misunderstood, should all give humanity serious food for thought. (p. 5)

Any child needs *liberty of internal development*. The child who is left at liberty to perform cognitive activities should find in his environment something organized in direct relation and unison to his internal organization that develops itself by natural laws, in the same way as a free insect finds in the form and qualities of flowers a direct correspondence between form and sustenance. Further Montessori holds that (cited in Oswald & Schulz-Benesch, 1997):

> The insect is undoubtedly free when, seeking the nectar which nourishes it, it is in reality helping the reproduction of the plant. There is nothing more marvelous in Nature than the correspondence between the organs of these two orders of beings destined to such a providential co-operation. The secret of the free development of the child consists, therefore, in organizing for him the means necessary for his internal nourishment, means corresponding to a primitive impulse of the child, comparable to that which makes the newborn infant capable of sucking milk from the breast, which by its external form and elaborated sustenance, corresponds perfectly to the requirements of the infant.
>
> It is in the satisfaction of this primitive impulse, this internal hunger, that the child's personality begins to organize itself and reveal its characteristics; just as the newborn infant, in nourishing itself, organizes its body and its natural movements. (pp. 11-12)

The fundamentals of Montessori's pedagogical approach are based on the following prerequisites:

- It is necessary to develop a child's initiative by providing the liberty of internal development. Any child is capable of self-directed cognitive activity, with the teacher or adult being an observer but who can help when needed and interfere if the learning situation requires it.
- A well-prepared environment enables children to independently perform various tasks and exercises, which arouses their motivation to creative activity.
- Children's cognitive activity is increased when they are absorbed by, and intensely concentrate on, the given activity. It is in learning to

recognize precious moments of concentration where the key to all pedagogy lies.

- Children should perform a great variety of observational activities requiring the use of all senses. In the light of this requirement, it becomes necessary to draw a specific attention to developing their small and gross motor skills.

The ideas she proposed and materials she developed are used not only in specially organized Montessori classrooms. Throughout the world democratically thinking pedagogues are on the way to implementing her ideas in classroom practice as well as in home schooling.

## LEV VYGOTSKY

I venture to begin this section by recalling a fragment of social contact occurred in the United States.

It happened at the University of New Mexico in Albuquerque in the fall of 1994. Professor Vera John-Steiner invited me to her office where I sat on a chair and immediately noticed on the wall the portrait of a man who seemed familiar to me.

"Oh," exclaimed I, "I see something familiar to me. It must be Vygotsky's picture"!

"Exactly, we consider him a classic and appreciate his teachings," said Vera John-Steiner.

By seeing a picture of my countryman, an adept who lived a short life but has left a galactic-size legacy, I was additionally instilled with confidence that Vygotsky's scientific and humanitarian heritage had begun gaining weight in the western hemisphere.

In our further interaction, we shared insights on the many psychological and pedagogical issues that this Russian adept had elaborated in his books. In the end she presented me with a copy of her article in which she based some of her assumptions on Vygotsky's ideas.

Lev Vygotsky (November 17, 1896- June 11, 1934) lived a short but fruitful life. In his youth, he was interested in literature, poetry, and philosophy and studied medicine and law at Moscow University. Even though he became interested in psychology only at the age of 28, he became one of the outstanding psychologists and pedagogues of all time. People involved in pedagogical psychology unanimously claim that, if any discussion in a field of teaching/learning is really serious, it is impossible to exclude Vygotsky's ideas from that discussion.

His contribution to psychology and education is virtually invaluable and enormous both in quality and quantity. The space of the article permits me to draw the reader's attention to only some of his basic pedagogical and psycho-linguistic assumptions.

As Vygotsky claimed, *solving the entire social problem* is eventually a prime objective in child development because cognitive skills and patterns of thinking have their origin in social relations and culture. Children gradually internalize the processes they use in social contexts and start using them independently. In all this scheme, interaction with peers and adults is an important means for promoting cognitive development.

While presenting one of his lectures at Moscow Pedagogical State University, Alexey Alexeevich Leontiev, a prominent Russian psychologist, linguist, and educator, whose father Alexey Nikolayevich Leontiev had been personally familiar with Vygotsky, explained to us the Vygotsky's idea of socialization in a much simpler way. He said, "A child should learn how to go out of the classroom into the corridor to interact with other peers, then, into the school yard, and from there, into a larger societal setting lying outside the school premises."

In cognitive development, *language plays an absolutely essential role.* Language is so closely interconnected with thought that the latter comes into existence through the former or, as Vygotsky holds, through word. Thought undergoes many changes before it turns into speech. A union of thought and word represents a *phenomenon of verbal thought.* The transition from thought to word occurs through meaning. Verbal thought is created in the following way: from a motive that engenders a thought to the shaping of the thought in the inner speech, then in the meaning of words, and ultimately, in words. In this mechanism, the thought can be compared to a "cloud shedding a shower of words." "What is contained in thought simultaneously is unfolding in speech successively" (Vygotsky, 1991, p. 91). Thought comes into existence through words, and eventually, the speech structures a child masters become the basic structures of his thinking and influence the way how the child perceives the surrounding reality. Words play a key role in the historical development of consciousness. Thus, human thinking is speech thinking.

Vygotsky believed that maximum cognitive development occurs when a child is provided with challenging tasks that the child cannot yet perform independently but can accomplish with a little help and guidance of a more competent individual. Such range of tasks is known as the *zone of proximal development*. This zone includes a child's learning and problem-solving abilities that are, for the time being, in an immature embryonic state and that are just beginning to develop. In other words, this zone is yet an empty sheet which should be filled with subsequent cognitive potential. Therefore, for enhancing proper cognitive development, it is beneficial to provide children with *attempting tasks* which are a little bit more difficult than the ones children can do independently.

Vygotsky's research in education and psychology has inspired numerous educational implications for contemporary educators. For example, a considerable number of school teachers use problem-solving techniques and methods based on posing challenging tasks in order to enhance students' developmental abilities "hidden" in the zone of proximal development.

Contemporary teachers use the *method of scaffolding*, which enables a learner to realize a task under the teacher's guidance. As soon as the learner becomes more proficient in performing the task, the teacher withdraws his or her support. Teachers unanimously acknowledge that scaffolding is an effective technique in promoting children's and adolescents' cognitive and creative potential.

Our discussion thus leads to several implications for educators.

## Study the Pedagogical Ideas of Five Illustrious and All-Time Classics

Enrich your professional horizons by studying the life paths, biographies, pedagogical ideas, and creative legacies of John Comenius, who blazed pioneering trails in education; Leo Tolstoy, who was an advocate of the principle of freedom in educating the young; John Dewey, who promoted pragmatic principles in educational settings; Maria Montessori, whose creed was based on providing the liberty of children's internal development; and Lev Vygotsky, who thought that cognitive skills and ways of thinking have their origin in social relations and culture. Upon scrupulous analysis of their ideas, creeds, admonitions, their creative activity, and their overall contribution into education, child development, and humanitarian thought, one can deduce that the essence of their pedagogical legacy has many features in common. All five theorists were born, in many ways, "ahead of time."

These five intellectuals unanimously shared the important idea of the necessity of developing children's inner capabilities, promoting their motivation to cognitive activity, and of enhancing their initiative. In child development the role of the teacher is great, but the teacher alone cannot solve all problems in children's intellectual, sociocultural, and physical development. It is worthwhile to know that any child has a "teacher within himself;" therefore most of the problems he can solve *by himself;* other problems--with a little assistance from a teacher or adult.

These five pedagogues, both explicitly and implicitly, recognized a cognitive activity as consisting of at least the following stages: observation, critical interpretation of what has been observed, putting forward plans to materialize the formulated task, the realization of the task, and the evaluation of what has been realized.

The prominent personalities and reformists whose creative careers I have examined:

- were progressive in their thinking, designing, and implementing educational ideas, methods, and ways of teacher-student interaction;
- were strong proponents of student-centered rather than subject-centered teaching;
- sought better ways of educating children and refining human society;
- believed that education is a social process, stressed the necessity and importance of the proper socialization of children and adolescents, and claimed that any individual must become a good member of human society.

According to their stand in the world and according to their pedagogical creed, these distinguished educators and humanists have ignited bright sparks and electrified the souls of educators throughout the world to further improving and advancing the matters of education and child-rearing.

## Follow Vygotsky's Wise Admonitions

In promoting a child's cognitive growth, remember Lev Vygotsky's recommendations about the importance of providing a child with a new task that should be a little bit more problematic than previous ones, thus orienting this new task into the not-yet-utilized area of cognitive development or as Vygotsky said--into the zone of proximal development. You should assist the child, but much depends on the child's initiative, on the degree of the little one's ability to independently contact with the objects in the environment and the ability to feel himself a growing human being.

## Investigate and Benefit from the Legacy of Other Distinguished Educators

Learn more about other renowned pedagogues and thinkers who were heroes of their historical epochs and whose ideas and principles have considerably influenced modern educational theories and practices. Following is brief information on some of them (Piskunov, 2005).

- Jean-Jacques Rousseau (1712-1778), a Swiss philosopher, enlightener, and pedagogue who advocated the idea that education should promote the development of children's inner faculties endowed by nature. He postulated that freedom is one of the most important rights of man, and the role of an educator is to develop a child's capabilities without excessive exterior compulsion.
- Johann Heinrich Pestalozzi (1767-1835), a Swiss pedagogue whose educational ideas have enormously impacted the global humanitarian and pedagogical thought. He considered that education should be child-centered and based on a child's self-activity.
- Wilhelm von Humboldt (1769-1859), a German philosopher and linguist who contributed greatly to reforming the Prussian educational system. He stressed the idea that individuals should always educate themselves and, at the same time, contribute to ameliorating the surrounding world.
- Adolph Diesterweg (1790-1866), one of the most renowned German educators and thinkers who sought to reorganize moral and social aspects of education. He advocated the secularization of educational institutions and professionalization of teachers.
- Konstantin Ushinsky (1824-1871), a distinguished Russian pedagogue who maintained that child development should be based on using folk pedagogical and cultural traditions of people. He also supported the idea of using the results of anthropological sciences (psychology, history, philosophy, anatomy, and physiology) in educating children and adolescents.

Today we are witnessing the emergence of numerous novel and experimental strategies of teaching and teacher-student and parent-child interaction. In the light of such progressive breakthroughs, some of the philosophical and pedagogical ideas of these pedagogues may seem outmoded and hackneyed, especially in the eyes of those educators and theorists who obsessively support the ideas of the excessive use of technology in education. I assume that all educators in general support the idea of using computers and related machinery. But I am of a strong opinion that the applications of digital and other technological devices can *only assist in and facilitate* (not always in correct humanitarian direction) cognitive development of children. However, such devices and the virtual reality they create can not lie at the core of human thinking and serve as an ideal springboard and foundation for child development.

Thus, what is important for us, educators, researchers, and academics of this new and roaring epoch is that the *creative activity and legacy* of these and other classics of education *made and are still making* a considerable contribution to ameliorating the global educational space. What these *mental giants* planted years ago has grown up, profusely blossoms, and yields plentiful healthy fruit with each newly-emerging decade.

It becomes important to revisit the pedagogical legacy of noted educators and thinkers and seek novel ways in educating children basing on the ideas of those adepts and taking into consideration contemporary innovative strategies. Many educators discharge such responsibilities well. At the same time, one detrimental tendency keeps creeping up: Children and adolescents are becoming indifferent to reading the conventional printed text. Let us talk about this problem in the section to come.

*Chapter 12*

# WHY DON'T STUDENTS READ ANYMORE?

*A house without books is like a room without windows.*
Heinrich Mann

*This will never be a civilized country until we expend*
*more money for books than we do for chewing gum.*
Elbert Hubbard

Educators and parents confess that most children and young adults have become indifferent to reading books. Some of them rarely open their textbooks, reference literature or journals and newspapers. The situation is somewhat analogous with college and university students. To this, many people give a simple answer: Young people have reduced their motivation to reading because they can satisfy their cognitive and aesthetic needs by easier ways--through television and computer (Internet) channels. However, should educators, teacher educators, and parents be indifferent to this fact and sit twiddling their thumbs? *They should not!*

Some young people have started forgetting renowned classics--writers and poets of the past. They have also lost impetus to reading present-day authors. I will briefly recall five noted personalities whose literary legacy is worth becoming familiar with.

# WILLIAM SHAKESPEARE

He was born in Stratford-upon-Avon on April 23, 1564. He attended the grammar school and received the best schooling that was available in Stratford at that time. He had no experience of a university, which in fact was a positive advantage for him. Some of his "contemporaries who prided themselves of their learning have since been criticized for artificiality, whereas Shakespeare had enough education to profit from it, but not so much that it spoiled him" (Parker, 2007, p. 6). He began his career as an actor and playwright with a London theatrical company in the 1590s. After staying in London for approximately 22 years, he returned to his native town, where he bought a house known as New Place. His creative legacy includes 37 plays, 4 poems, and 154 sonnets (Varlamova, 2003b). He died on his birthday, April 23, 1616, and was buried in Holy Trinity Church where he had been baptized 52 years earlier.

Shakespeare's legacy is huge and eternal. His depictions of human life have meaning for other people because life had a special meaning for him. He depicted history, love, tragedy, and comedy by seeing the surrounding life as it is, in its beauty and ugliness, its harmony and chaos. Michael Parker (2007) writes:

> William Shakespeare lived according to his own text--a man of many parts, and a man for all the world. Each generation in turn since his death seems to have found some new, distinct quality in his plays that meets its concerns or catches its preoccupations. In the 19th century he was valued above all for his characters, such as Falstaff and Hamlet, which expressed a rich variety of human life in terms that appealed to a robustly romantic age. During World War II, it was Shakespeare the patriot that fired the minds of struggling Englishmen... More recently, we have found unfathomed depths in the beauty of his poetry. (p. 1)

His birth place is annually visited by a large number of sightseers and tourists. I also visited his home town and made a sightseeing tour about its historical places.

> Stratford-upon-Avon is now a beautiful town lying 22 miles south east of Birmingham. Undoubtedly, among the main sights of town are the places related to Shakespeare's life. First of all, it is the house in Henley Street where he was born. Then, there is Nash's House in Chapel Street,

in which his granddaughter Elizabeth lived. With a feeling of trepidation did I enter Holy Trinity Church where Shakespeare is buried in its chancel next to his wife Anna Hathaway and daughter Susanna.

There are also other attractions in Stratford such as Swan Theater, the Armories, the Butterfly Farm, and the Avonbank Garden. I stood for a while near the Royal Shakespeare Theater, which was built in 1932 and replaced much later by a new auditorium. In this theater, the playing actors and the audience can share the same space, as in the time when Shakespeare's plays were first performed. While walking through the streets and along the riverbank, I constantly felt the presence of Shakespeare's spirit

Shakespeare's works sadden, entertain, enlighten, teach, and, most importantly, educate.

To most earthlings, his name is immediately associated with his celebrated phrase "To be or not to be: that is the question" from *Hamlet* (the actual title is *The Tragedy of Hamlet, Prince of Denmark*). This saying seems applicable in a great variety of serious and ordinary, day-to-day situations, but the deepest meaning of it is eternal and, I may add, prophetic. This is probably the best-known saying in all world literature.

## ALEXANDRE DUMAS PERE

The author whose stories have been translated into almost a hundred languages was born on July 24, 1802. His mother told him interesting stories about his father's bravery during the years of Napoleon I, which inspired young Alexandre's imagination for adventure. At age 20 he moved to Paris and began writing for magazines and plays for theaters. Later he turned to writing novels. Dumas' writing activity earned him a great amount of money, but he spent lavishly on sumptuous living. He built a large château that was often full of his acquaintances and strangers who took advantage of his generosity. In 1851 he went to Belgium and, from there, to Russia, where he spent two years. He died on December 5, 1870 (Rapogov, 2004; "Alexandre," 2012).

In 2002 French President Jacque Chirac had his body exhumed and transported to the Panthéon of Paris. In his ceremonial speech President said: "With you, we were D'Artagnan, Monte Cristo, or Balsamo, riding along the roads of France, touring battlefields, visiting palaces and castles--with you, we dream" (cited in "Alexandre," 2012, p. 3).

Dumas is one of the most widely read French authors in the world. He was a novelist, a dramatist, and a prolific writer of non-fiction. His being a good cook also encouraged him to write *Grand Dictionnaire de cuisine* (Grand Dictionary of Cuisine). His stories gave producers the enthusiasm to create over 200 motion pictures. For example, the book *Les Trois Mousquetaires* (The Three Musketeers) has been filmed in several countries. Especially popular was and still is the version released by French-Italian film-makers in 1961. This two-part movie is considered by the critics and moviegoers to be the best filming of this great book. This movie appeared in Russia's cinema houses in the mid-1960s and instantaneously captured the imagination of, and created a furor among, teenagers all over the country. In fact, the movie appealed to the tastes of people of all ages. Among teenagers, the excitement caused by the movie lasted until the 1970s and even longer. In my teenhood, like most of the boys in our school, I was also captivated by this movie. We used to play a game called *Musketeers* on Sundays. I will try to recollect one of those many Sundays.

One Saturday afternoon, after classes, someone in the school corridor cried out loud, "Let's play musketeers this Sunday!" This incentive was heartily met with many "yeses." Following this call, on Sunday morning, two dozens boys from our school gathered on a field in the outskirts of Belebey, a town where I had been born and gone to school. The boys were "fully armed." Each had a sword made of wood and was wearing a protective vest. As a rule, we used to make swords ourselves. We did not have shields, because the musketeers who had lived in the 17th-century France had had none.

With all boys gathered, we divided into two teams of musketeers--the "Team of the King" and the "Team of Cardinal Richelieu"--and "fought" with each other crossing swords. Both teams "engaged in a battle" crying out "all for one, one for all," a motto that was, according to the book's content, first used by D'Artagnan. After a while, the Team of the King was victorious. It meant that, during the clash, all the musketeers of the other team had received a blow with a sword on the chest.

In what we did was nothing serious; it was just a play, nothing more. The blows we delivered were slight and not harmful. Throughout my "musketeer's career," I do not remember injuring someone or someone causing damage to my face or body with a sword, except for minor bruises I occasionally got by falling on the ground or on heaps of snow.

We had no professional coaches, except for some senior boys who often helped us to acquire some simple techniques of using the word. To tell the truth, we did not need any coaches. For example, my senior cousin Matveev Valerie, who attended the same school and who excelled in using the sword, taught me different techniques of how to effectively attack an "opponent" and defend myself.

Our practice in fencing was a health-enhancing enterprise. First, we played this game in the open. Second, we learned how to endure and overcome difficulties. Third, prior to a game, on week-days, each of us used to do various physical exercises and practiced in fencing with some other boy to be in shape during our Sunday games. Regular exercising developed our muscular and cardiovascular systems.

Dumas lived in Russia only for two years, but he has left a tremendous legacy, a tiny part of which I did experience by body and mind.

## ROBERT LOUIS STEVENSON

When our group of tourists was on a walking tour in Edinburgh, the guide stopped us at 17 Heriot Row.

"In this house," she said, "Robert Louis Stevenson grew up from the age of six and left it in 1880. He was actually born on November 13, 1850, in this city. In his childhood he suffered chronic health problems..." I was listening to her and simultaneously recalling the legendary personages from *Treasure Island*: Jim Hawkins, a young adventure-seeker; Captain Smollett, a brave seafarer; Long John-Silver, a pirate with a pet parrot called Captain Flint; and the mysterious island where the treasure had been buried. Later, a man from our group told me that the one legged John Silver's prototype was Stevenson's friend William Henley who, suffering from tuberculosis of the bone, had his left leg amputated in the late 1860s. While standing near the house, I also quickly brought to mind some main heroes from his novels *Kidnapped* and *The Black Arrow*.

In addition to all this, quite of a sudden, I visualized the scene displayed in front of the hotel Treasure Island in Las Vegas with two vessels standing on the water and with the houses symbolizing an old British seashore town in the background. The people who had designed and built this hotel and this "literary piece of British history" immortalized the novel and the adventuresome time when its heroes set sail in search of treasure and further popularized the name of Robert Stevenson himself in this entertainment city.

In 1867 Stevenson entered Edinburgh University as a science student, but had much more of a romantic nature at heart. He decided to pursue writing. His chronic illness prompted him to travel in the countries and places with a more mild and favorable climate. In his first books he described some of these trips. Between 1880 and 1887, he lived in different places abroad. In 1883 his book *Treasure Island* was published, which immediately made him famous. In 1888, accompanied by his wife, his step-son, and his mother, Louis Stevenson set sail for the South Seas. Eventually, enchanted by the life in the new places, he bought an estate in Apia, an island in Samoa. The local people lavished care and attention upon him. He lived there until his death on December 3, 1894 (Varlamova, 2003a; "Robert Louis," 2012).

Stevenson is one of the most translated authors of the world. At university, one of my majors was foreign literature. I read some of his novels in Russian, then, I read the same works in English. It was the sweetest reading I had ever had. I had a brilliant possibility to compare two languages and how they express the same phenomena and events. This reading enormously enriched my linguistic competency.

His novels and short stories are devoted to different events and themes. In *Prince Otto,* a comedy unfolds in an imaginary German principality; in *The Strange Case of Dr Jekyll and Mr Hyde,* a London lawyer investigates strange occurrences between two individuals; in *Kidnapped*, the boy, David Balfour, pursues his inheritance; in *The Master of Ballantrae,* the scenes develop in a range of countries; and in *The Black Arrow,* the reader is taken back to the time of the War of Roses.

# VIRGINIA HAMILTON

Virginia Esther Hamilton was born on March 12, 1934, and grew up amid an extended family in Yellow Springs, Ohio. She received a full scholarship to Antioch College in Yellow Springs, and in 1956 transferred to the Ohio State University in Columbus where she majored in literature and creative writing. She studied fiction writing at the New School for Social Research. In 1960 she married poet Arnold Adoff. They built and settled in a house in Yellow Springs. She died on February 19, 2002. Some of her works have been published posthumously.

Virginia Hamilton wrote and published 41 books in her lifetime. She won numerous awards in youth literature. Among them are (1) the Hans Christian Andersen Award for Writing, the highest international recognition bestowed on an author or illustrator of children's literature; (2) a MacArthur Fellowship; (3) the Laura Ingalls Wilder Award for her contribution to literature for children; and (4) The University of Southern Mississippi de Grummond Medal for lifetime achievement in children's literature ("Biography," 2012).

Her creative heritage is rather large. Below I enumerate just a few of her works ("Virginia's books", 2012):

- *Plain City* (1993). Among the people of different social and cultural background, Buhlaire Sims is ready to get some answers about her family.
- *Her Stories: African American Folktales, Fairy Tales, and True Tales* (1995). This collection spans the generations (from girl child to elder woman) in interesting stories ranging from Cinderella fantasy to folktales.
- *Second Cousins* (1998). A family reunion brings together two second cousins from New York.
- *Time Pieces: The Book of Times* (2001). In this semi-autobiographical novel, Hamilton weaves together the present time and the time of slavery.

# Simon J. Ortiz

One of the leading figures in the Native American renaissance, Simon Ortiz, was born in Albuquerque on May 27, 1941, and raised in the Acoma Pueblo village of McCartys (called *Deetseyamah* in the Acoma language). He wrote about his childhood years the following: "Within our clan--the Eagles--our family was close and supportive of each other, which was common throughout the Pueblo" (Ortiz, 1992, p. 6). He attended McCartys Day School, St. Catherine's Indian School in Santa Fe, and Grants High School. After serving in the U.S. Army, Ortiz enrolled at the University of New Mexico and, since 1968, taught at various institutions.

His literary career is associated with poetry, although he is also productive as a short story writer and essayist. His poetry depicts the importance of individual origins and journeys and grows out of his experience with the

Pueblo landscape and indigenous culture. He points out that the land should not be a property to be used. It is and must be a life-force to be respected ("Native voices," 2011). His poetry is saturated with oral tradition about which Ortiz (1992) writes in his autobiographical sketch:

> The oral tradition of Native American people is based upon spoken language, but it is more than that too. Oral tradition is inclusive; it is the actions, behavior, relationships, and practices throughout the whole social, economic, and spiritual life process of people. In this respect, the oral tradition is the consciousness of the people. I think at times 'oral tradition' is defined too strictly in terms of verbal-vocal manifestations in stories, songs, meditations, ceremonies, ritual, philosophies, and clan and tribal histories passed from older generations to the next. When I consider the 'idea' of Acoma oral tradition, I think of the interaction of the grandfather with his grandson, as well as what he spoke and what the story verbalizes as it is told. Oral tradition evokes and expresses a belief system, and it is specific activity that confirms and coveys that belief. (p. 7)

In the same sketch Simon Ortiz writes about visiting Laguna Elementary School and speaking to young students. Luckily, thanks to my colleagues from the University of New Mexico, Dr. Joseph Suina and Dr. Quincy Spurlin, on September 14, 1994, I was also happy to visit this same school.

> On the day of our visit to Laguna Elementary, there was an open house in this educational institution. The school principal Mary Ann Apodaca introduced the teachers to the parents. Joseph Suina also addressed the audience. After the formal part, there was an informal interaction between the school staff, parents, and students. I made acquaintance with Deborah Abrams, Lois Wacondo, Chris Oberholser and other educators. We saw beautiful articles and toys that students had manufactured themselves. I remember marveling at small brontosaurs and dinosaurs that a fifth-grader had made of clay.
>
> Joseph Suina and the school teachers introduced me to the overall atmosphere of the school. The school administration and educators had created a favorable environment for students to achieve academically and to socialize as citizens of a larger society. There were spacious classrooms, wide corridors, a good-looking library, and a grandiose gymnasium in the school. The library contained a huge number of books and teaching aids.

On the way back to Albuquerque, Joseph and Quincy told me a lot about the specificities of education in New Mexico and about the essence of multicultural education. I also came to learn that Joseph himself had worked at Laguna Elementary for two years in the 1970s.

I often read some of Simon Ortiz's poems in his book *Woven Stone,* which was presented to me by Dr. Richard van Dongen at the University of New Mexico. I also often remember my visits to the marvelous places in New Mexico where the Indian past and present embodies harmonious oneness, which is so vivid and so robust.

I end this chapter by urging educators to keep to the following suggestions:

## Encourage Students' Impetus to Reading

Impress on students the importance of reading the literature of the classics of the past and of present-day writers and poets. Students may refer to the creative legacy of William Shakespeare, who has introduced a lot of purely Shakespearean in poetry and expanded the beauty of the English language by inventing thousands of words; Alexandre Dumas, who was not only a great writer but also an adventurous traveler and a dedicated cook; Louis Stevenson, whose novels are full of adventure; Virginia Hamilton, who has substantially contributed to the field of African American literature; and Simon Ortiz, whose writing includes inspiring poems, wise essays, interesting short stories, and books for children and young adults.

## Focus Students' Attention on Other Noted Writers and Poets

Engage students in the reading and exploration of the creative legacy of other authors. Following are some of them.

- Earnest Hemingway (1889-1961), an American novelist, essayist, and short-story teller who liked to depict soldiers, hunters and other brave people. I remember analyzing his famous book *The Old Man and the Sea* during my final examination at the University.
- Maxine Kumin (b. 1925), an American poet who is also the author of four novels and numerous children's books.

- Mem Fox (b. 1946), an Australian writer of children's books. She has received a great number of rewards over the years.
- Candy Boyd Dawson (b. 1946), an American author of books for children and young adults.

Reading is not only gaining knowledge and information in the possible fastest way; a genuine form of reading makes a reader take to heart the fates of the characters and the events being depicted and, often, to live the lives of the literary personages. A good fairy-tale, story, or novel makes an educative impact on young readers. A good article in a scientific journal may arouse a student's impetus to deeper understand the surrounding world. A science-fiction story or novel may help develop the student's imagination and scope. In fact, any story, novel, or scientific article with a decent and morally favorable content is likely to positively influence children's and adolescents' cognitive and socioemotional development.

Young girls and boys have begun to enslave themselves by navigating in the virtual world, and they have cooled to reading books, magazines, and newspapers. They strive to freedom and aspire to conquer the world. At the same time, they increasingly compromise their health by their own behaviors. In such circumstances, promoting children's and adolescents' health remains an uppermost objective of educators and parents. The following chapter will contain more about it.

*Chapter 13*

# LACK OF HEALTH EDUCATION

*An ounce of prevention is worth a pound of cure.*
Benjamin Franklin

*The art of medicine consists*
*of amusing the patient while Nature cures the disease.*
Voltaire

The English proverb "Health is above wealth" clearly indicates that health is a priority in human society. When someone falls ill, his former identity is lost and he becomes *another* person. He may lose heart, remain stressed for some period of time, and even lose hope of returning to a previous healthy state. Especially sad is the suffering of young girls and boys afflicted with physical and psychic ailments. I define health education as a process aimed at teaching students about health, how to escape health-compromising behaviors, how to prevent various diseases, and how to live and behave in a health-promoting manner. Many diseases in children and adolescents have multiple causes. On one hand, it is impossible to make schools and educators fully responsible for children's health; on the other, they must not stand aside.

The past three decades have been witnessing a decline in schoolchildren's health. In addition, a process of the rejuvenation of diseases is now parading across continents. A considerable number of children and adolescents come down with diseases which in the past troubled people only closer to their 50s and 60s.

# HEALTH DISORDERS

*Heart Diseases.* A cardiovascular disease emerges when one's heart and blood vessels do not pump properly. There may be congenital heart diseases (caused by hereditary factors) and acquired heart diseases. The most widely spread heart conditions in children are structural heart defects.

*Diabetes.* There are two types of diabetes: Type 1 diabetes, caused by the inability of the pancreas to produce insulin, and   type 2 diabetes, when the pancreas can still produce insulin, but the insulin functions abnormally. The most common form of diabetes in children is type 1 diabetes.

*Cancer.* Childhood cancers are known to have different profile from adult cancers. The most common children's cancers are leukemia, lymphoma, brain tumors, and soft tissue sarcoma. For instance, in leukemia, the cancer attacks the white blood cells; lymphomas arise in the lymphatic system.

*Eating Disorders.* Triggered by physiological, sociocultural, and behavioral factors, eating disorders lead to eating habits that can result in serious health problems. The three major types of eating disorders are *anorexia nervosa* (the relentless pursuit of thinness through reduction of food intake), *bulimia nervosa* (overeating food that follows by self-inducing vomiting or laxative use), and *binge eating* (eating a large amount of food without purging).

*Sexually Transmitted Diseases (STDs).* STDs are spread by intimate contact: by vaginal intercourse as well as by anal-genital and oral-genital contacts. Sexually active adolescents, especially those who practice unprotected sex, have the highest rate of STDs. Most common among teenagers are chlamydia, gonorrhea, trichomoniasis, and genital herpes. The incidences of syphilis and HIV/AID are also on the rise among adolescents. Studies indicate that STDs began affecting not only adolescents but also children at an earlier age.

# SPECIAL HEALTH CONDITIONS

Some students have ongoing, long-term health conditions such as chronic illnesses, physical disabilities, and mental problems. These disorders may be a result of genetic, environmental and other specific factors.

*Chronic diseases* are long-term conditions. Some affect children for a few years; others may linger on into adulthood. Asthma is a chronic disease, and the number of asthma-affected children and adolescents continues to grow. Cystic fibrosis is another chronic ailment, usually inherited. It affects mainly the respiratory system but also the liver and the digestive system. Some children suffer from attention-deficit/hyperactivity disorder, a chronic disease creating problems and difficulties in their cognitive processing. Children also suffer from cold-related diseases such as pharyngitis, laryngitis, sinus infection, upper respiratory tract infection, and bronchitis. Some of these disorders may develop into long-term forms.

Children with *physical disabilities* have the same fundamental needs as normal children. Some students with physical impairments have both physical and cognitive problems; but, on the whole, many others have the same cognitive, socioemotional, and intellectual abilities as the rest of learners.

Many problems arise for parents and educators when they have to cope with children suffering from *mental disorders.* The most common mental illnesses in children are anxiety disorder, pervasive development disorders, eating disorders, elimination disorders, learning and communication disorders, affective (mood) disorders, schizophrenia, and tic disorders. Mental illnesses can be triggered by hereditary, biological, environmental, and psychological factors. Mental health issues are becoming a problem of global concern. It is estimated that by 2020 depression may become one of the most burdensome illnesses (Carter, 1999).

Children and adolescents are vulnerable to *viral pandemics and bacterial infections* if they do not take a good care of themselves and neglect preventive measures. A wide-spread disease is influenza, which is transmitted through the air and contact with contaminated surfaces. It usually spreads in seasonal epidemics. The death tall from flu is rather high. Annually it claims up to 500,000 people worldwide. History remembers the 1918-1919 Spanish flu pandemic that killed up to 100 million people. By mutation or by reassortment of genetic material, new flu viruses continually involve. Influenza may have severe after-effects. A frequent after-effect of flu is bacterial pneumonia. In other cases, it can precipitate respiratory, kidney, or cardiovascular diseases.

As for bacteria, they may be both harmless and dangerous. For example, tuberculosis is one of the hazardous bacterial diseases. Today it becomes rather difficult to combat bacterial diseases. Bacteria have "developed" a resistance to almost every antibiotic developed. Maryn McKenna (2011) writes:

Bacteria, after all, have evolution on their side. It takes them 20 minutes to produce a new generation. It takes a decade or more to research and develop a new drug... With no new medications in the pipeline capable of dispatching these latest superbugs, we may have to live with the risk of untreatable infections for an uncomfortably long time. (p. 30)

Looking ahead, researches envision the emergence of completely resistant strains of gram-negative bacteria, arriving long before the drugs that could treat them. (p. 33)

## HEALTH COMPROMISING BEHAVIORS

Many children and teenagers compromise their health by their own behaviors. *Cigarette smoking* is a most widespread health-compromising behavior among both boys and girls. It increases the risk of developing chronic bronchitis, tuberculosis, lung cancer and other diseases. In general, smoking makes a negative impact on all the bodily systems.

A serious problem detrimental to health and the surrounding society is *drug abuse,* which causes not only physiological damage to people but also leads to their sexual and moral decline. Despite tough and determined measures to combat drug production, trafficking, and use, abuse of illegal and prescription drugs causes accidental deaths from overdoses, drug-related diseases, and gang crime. Another serious health and social hazard is *alcohol abuse.* Because alcoholic beverages, especially beer, are so common, people forget that alcohol is also a drug and that getting used to it is as easy as getting used to cocaine or marihuana. A starting point of becoming a heavy drinker or alcoholic, as the drinking public admits, may begin with drinking beer. Therefore, it is heart-rending to see how much of that yellow liquid is consumed by high school and college students. Sadly, the number of young beer-lovers is climbing rapidly in many countries.

Basing on findings of medical science and my observations of human experience, I am ready to repeat millions of times that alcohol and drug abuse are both extremely hazardous for school and college age children, especially for young females, who normally become intoxicated faster and become alcoholics or heavy drug users in a shorter period. Both alcohol and drug use do not spare anyone, despite the age, gender, ethnicity, and social status. Alcoholism and drug dependencies are self-destructive and mind-altering diseases. Closely aligned with drug and alcohol abuse are juvenile delinquency, teenage pregnancy, school absenteeism, and school dropout.

Moreover, alcohol use and drug abuse closely align with early, inordinate, and unprotected *sexual activity*. An upsurge of sexual activity promotes a further rise of moral degradation. Prostitution involving school- and college-age girls and even boys is one of its manifestations. Unprotected sexual pleasures discharged under the influence of drugs and alcohol make direct inroads into early pregnancy and STDs. Early sexual activity, in turn, aligns with alcohol and drug use and risky behaviors. Early and active sexual activity may also lead to a psychic deformation of an individual. Evidence suggests that American adolescents living in low-income neighborhoods are often more sexually active and have higher pregnancy rates than those living in more affluent circumstances. African American adolescents tend to engage in sexual relations at an earlier age than the representatives of other ethnic groups; whereas Asian American adolescents "have the most restrictive timetable" (Santrock, 2002, p. 356).

One more problem affecting children's health results from their inability to *cope with extreme climatic conditions* (Sinagatullin, 2009b). There are places on earth with relatively mild and favorable climate, such as the southeastern United States, France, Italy, or southern Ukraine. Other regions, especially in Alaska, northern Canada, northern European countries, and northeastern Russia, experience long and cold winters. In cold periods, some children often refuse to wear headgear and warm clothes. As a result, they frequently catch colds and develop more serious cold-related diseases. Conversely, in the places with hot climate, such as southern United States, Mexico, and Australia, people of all ages are subjected to sun-related diseases, especially skin cancer.

## WHO IS A HEALTHY PERSON?

Intriguing as it is, this question may be looked at differently across cultures. For example, in Western cultures, an ideal healthy male is depicted as muscular, tall, and possibly armed with physical self-defense techniques, like the famous Belgian-born actor Jean-Claude Van Dame or the legendary American-born actor Steven Seagal. A perfect female is portrayed as slim and tall, like the renowned American actress and model Uma Thurman and the Australian-born siren Nicole Kidman. But this information may confuse students from Asian and Latin American cultures, who are normally shorter.

Students who are overweight owing to some illness or stout by nature may also feel uncomfortable when robust males and slim females are depicted and talked about in mass media. In my opinion, the category of man's beauty should not be associated only will facial and bodily features. Beauty is known to be revealed both in human beings' external and internal characteristics.

According to modern Western medicine, eating healthy food and, at the same time, preventing any possible and yet-undiscovered ailment is associated with consumption of vitamin-reach, low-fat, and low-calorie food. In some cases, medical science recommends reducing meat products. But these suggestions may be incongruent with some healthy or national food concepts characteristic of specific ethnic, cultural, and religious groups. For instance, fatty pork and lard are favorite national foods in Ukrainian and Russian communities. Consumption of meat and fatty soup or bouillon is a normal, almost daily practice among rural Kazakhs, Bashkirs, and Tatars. Eating pork, beef, and chicken is a common practice in Czech Republic. In general, Czech traditional food may be "considered fatty and heavy for health" by the people who come from other countries. I frequently came across the following list of dishes on the menus of Czech restaurants and cafes: smoked ribs, roast smoked seasoned pig knee, duck breast, roast pork, and marinated beef sirloin. In addition, such dishes may be often followed by a beer--a national drink in Czech Republic.

When we touch upon the issues of a balanced use of calorie-rich food, much depends on the type of profession a person is involved in. For people involved in sedentary professions, consumption of great quantities of fat and sugar-rich food is not desirable, whereas people whose occupation is based on physical labor or who are actively involved in sports need more calories in their daily meals.

Even though the mainstream medicine recommends its own, so-called scientifically proven recipes against different diseases, culture-related preventive and healing practices may differ across cultures. In Russia's Tatar and Bashkir communities, there is a strong belief in the healing and majestic power of meat bouillon. Symbolically, this approach may be called "bouillon medicine." Among ethnic Russians and many other ethnic groups inhabiting Russia, honey is an iconic remedy, and, in various forms, recommended for almost all ailments. Let us say, that Russians use "honey medicine." As some ethnic and cultural groups in Southeast Asia often use various balms, their practice of using such substances may be referred to as "balm medicine."

People living in the Mediterranean region believe in the health-promoting capacities of olive oil and not in vain! Medical science confirms that olive oil cuts risk of heart disease, fights cancers, wards off arthritis, keeps diabetes at bay, stops pain, beats bone loss, and defends against HIV (Orey, 2009). The list of recipes can be longer. Not only in the symbolic terms but in real sense of the words can we say that Mediterranean countries use "olive oil medicine." I brought the knowledge about the brilliant possibilities of olive oil from Rome, where I had first seen people dipping a piece of bread into olive oil and pushing it into their mouth cavities with their eyes pleasurably closed.

Since prehistoric times peoples all over the world have been using plants, mushrooms, and other products of soil for preventing and treating various health disorders. Such practices are referred to as "herbal medicine." For instance, most of my relatives and people surrounding me often use different herbs against colds and other ailments. In the summertime, I like to collect some therapeutic herbs which my family members then add to their diet in the form of herbal tea to prevent colds or boost the immune system.

## "NEGLIGENCE OF OURSELVES"

The subtitle sounds strange. *How* and *why* can we, reasoning beings, neglect ourselves? I will try to prove that we *can* and we *do*. What substance prevails in our bodies? *Water!* I will not be mistaken if I say that we consist of water! We seem to disregard this fact. We automatically drink anything possible: commercial non-alcoholic liquids such as lemonade and cola as well as alcoholic drinks such as beer, whisky, and wine. By doing so we alter and modify the water content of our bodies for the worse. Our cells "swimming in the pristine near-cell bouillon" are continually struggling against the unclear liquid that we consume. How *strong* are our cells to withstand a life-long impact of dirty liquids!

Water is "blue gold" in the economic sense of the word and "golden liquid" in terms of physiology and health. It is one of the most important health-enhancing substances. As water is what we consist of, by drinking it we "add ourselves to our bodies," we maintain our physical structures in good order, and we, by consuming this golden liquid, cleanse the body of waste and toxins.

Governments and global health-promoting organizations can do a great deal to address the issues of students' health.

## Global Health Promotion Activities

Every child on the surface of earth is a treasure of humankind. We must take care of each young man's and woman's health. Health like many other essential issues in our lives should be a matter of global concern. It stands to reason that educators should also be healthy.

It becomes important for global, regional, and governmental health-promoting organizations and institutions to organize health promotion and disease prevention activities. It is necessary to develop and disseminate useful information for the people across cultures to understand the meaning of being healthy in human society. There also should be a multicultural understanding and evaluation of health promotion programs and related initiatives. Governments should allocate robust financial resources for health promotion programs within their own countries. These measures will undoubtedly pay manifold dividends.

Having discussed some vital problems concerning children's health, I offer some general strategies for educators:

## Renew Your Knowledge on Medicine

Enhance your knowledge-base on the new achievements in the health and medical fields. Times change swiftly! For example, some diseases such as diabetes, cancer, and a variety of heart diseases have rejuvenated and are now striking people at a younger age. Some remedies that proved efficacious a decade ago are not effective today. There is also a noticeable trend to using folk health-promoting methods across cultures, even though folk medicine was and is still denied by zealots of official medicine.

## Study Students' Family Health Histories

Collect information and data about your students by investigative their genealogical trees, including their parents, grandparents, and relatives. If needed, share this information with other teachers and heath professionals. A family health history can tell you many things about risk factors for diabetes, cancer and others diseases. A pattern of disease in a family may be a definite sign of some sort of an inherited disease passed on from one generation to another. In case a child does not have a history of a disease, he can still be at risk of contracting the disease owing to environmental factors or health-compromising behaviors. A person cannot change his or her genes, but it is quite possible to change lifestyles and behaviors leading to certain diseases.

## Empower Children to Explore Their Bodies

Help each student learn as much as possible about his body and how it functions. Children may know well the essential parts of the computer and how it works. They may easily repair their bicycles because they know "what belongs to what." They can even know how to repair their photo and video cameras. But they seldom know well the specifics of their bodily parts. What happens with the air we breathe and, therefore, live? Where does the water we drink "go" and how is it spread inside the body? Where does the arterial blood take its beginnings? What is the difference between the arterial and venous blood? How do our gastrointestinal and cardiovascular systems function? Why is it important to be extremely cautious about our nervous system? Children study biology, but can we be sure that they remember these and other essential facts?

Much depends on how children themselves take care of their health. Early in life should they learn about major facts concerning their organism. After all, "their health is in their own hands."

## Take Care of Children's Eating Habits

Many children pursue wrong approaches to satisfying their gastronomic needs. They may not know that they should limit fast food and sugary drinks like sodas and sweetened juices. Eating too much sugar and fat is harmful to both children and adolescents. They should enrich their daily ration by consuming more fresh fruits and vegetables, all of which contain live cells and a variety of vitamins and minerals, so indispensable for their bodies and health. And they should drink more natural water.

## Teach Children to Take Care of Their Skin

When I was a school student, I did not possess sufficient knowledge about skin and how to protect it. I used to stay in the sun for hours without protecting

my head, face, and the whole body. The medical science of the 1970s
recommended a gradual process of becoming tanned: by starting from ten
minutes on the first day of sunbathing and increasing further portions by five
minutes each proceeding day. Nobody told me that long stays in the sun are
harmful. Today we are dealing with "another sun" and "another skies." A
severe one-time exposure to sun in adolescence can have consequences in
adulthood. What I say is not to suggest that school students should always
shun sun rays and stay in shade. Sun and its energy are vital for us all,
especially for the young and growing people. What I am driving at is that we,
educators, teacher educators, and parents, should educate children to wisely
and rationally use sun energy. As the incidence of skin cancers is increasing
throughout the world, it becomes important to develop children's sun-related
knowledge, promote a skin-diseases awareness, and to teach self-care skills.

## Provide Opportunities for Regular Exercising

Jogging, bicycling, walking, going on an excursion and engaging in other
sporting and physical activities are invaluable prerequisites for enhancing
children's health. Some parents deprive their children from active forms of
existence by taking them to schools and back home by car, even when they
live not far from the educational institution. It means that these children, who
"step" from the car to the school building in the morning and then step back
from the car to the thresholds of their houses in the afternoon, practically have
little possibility of deeply filling their lungs with fresh oxygen-containing air.
One can only imagine what harm such parents do to their kids. How is it
possible for a growing child to be healthy if his muscles do not experience a
sufficient shake-up? It is lack of exercising that may pave a direct path to
overweight, obesity and related problems.

A good way to keep oneself healthy and physically in shape is using a
bicycle. I myself had loved bicycling until the age 22. These days I prefer
walking to any possible place: to my office and back home, to a supermarket,
to my garden and other places. Some day I will probably "return" to bicycling.
Out of necessity and for pleasure, in some northern European countries and the
countries of Southeast Asian, people like riding bicycles. To my mind,
Holland is one of the most bicycle-crazy nations in the world. Their bicycles
outnumber the country's residents.

## Combat Substance Abuse

In cooperation with parents, pedagogical personnel, and medical services, organize concurrent measures to combat substance abuse among children and adolescents. It becomes necessary to implement and sustain anti-drug, anti-alcohol, and anti-smoking campaigns and continually provide young people with meaningful instruction about the real harm these substances bring to health. More joint efforts are needed to stop the cultivation, manufacture, sale, and use of narcotics.

## Reflect on the Importance of Golden Liquid

Help your students rethink their attitudes to the phenomenon of water. Next to the air one breathes, water is the most vital ingredient one's body needs and consists of. Many people, especially at a young age, seldom think of this fact. Others are completely unaware of water being so essential to the healthy functioning of man.

Our bodies use water in all cells, tissues, and organs. The amount of water we need depends on the climatic conditions we live in and how physically active we are. Water protects our tissues, spinal cord, and joints; helps our bodies remove waste; aids in digestion; and prevents us from becoming dehydrated (Laskey, 2008).

Let students know that consuming a sufficient amount of natural water can play an important role in keeping their physical and mental states healthy. Water helps prevent and treat a range of diseases. When we experience signs of fatigue and pain, it may mean that our bodies cry for water. In passing, I find it important to note that a person's daily intake of pure water should be taken with a proportional intake of natural salt. Water and salt are one inseparable whole (Batmanghelidj, 1995). Some medical workers persuade people of all ages to abstain from adding any salt at all to food. This is an unwise decision. The cells inside our body are "swimming in a relatively salty bouillon." To test it, it is just necessary to taste a drop of your sweat. Obviously, an excessive intake of salt--as well as the overdoing in consuming sugar--is inevitably harmful for our health.

## Love Your Children

You should respect and love your students irrespective of their ethnic and cultural background. Love is a most treasured phenomenon on earth and, probably, beyond earth too. Further, I add the fantastically inspiring excerpts from Peterim Sorokin (1991) to what I have already said about the phenomenon of love previously:

> In all its forms, love is one of the most important factors of good health and longevity. (p. 128)
>
> People deprived of warmth and love get sick and die as quickly as if they might have got sick and died from infections, hunger, or inappropriate diet. (p. 129)
>
> To love and to be loved is probably the most essential vitamin indispensable for a healthy growth of an individual and for a happy course of his life. (p. 131)

## Take Care of Your own Health

By admonishing pupils to health-promoting strategies, do not forget about your own health. Much of what has been recommended above is equally important to keep in mind for yourself. In other cases, read a good book on how to prevent diseases and keep your body and mind in good order. "Make friends" with a couple of good magazines on health issues. There is also a great deal of information on the topic in the Internet. Also, be prepared to render the first aid when your students or colleagues feel unwell or are injured.

A teacher cannot say, "Well, colleagues, last year I devoted a great amount of time to educating my pupils about their health; this year I will pay more attention to citizenship education." Our health *is* with us and *depends* on us. Therefore, teaching students to keep their health in good maintenance should be a non-stop process.

Educational institutions should pay more attention to promoting children's and teenagers' health and not forget to enhance their global competency. What is global education? How to develop students' global competency? For answers, let us delve into the forthcoming chapter.

# Chapter 14

# LACK OF GLOBAL EDUCATION

*I am not an Athenian, nor a Greek,*
*but a citizen of the world.*
Socrates

*The man who finds his country sweet is only a raw beginner;*
*the man for whom each country is as his own is already strong;*
*but only the man for whom the whole world is as a foreign country is*
*perfect.*
St. Victor

Globalization and its relation to education is one of the most discussed-of problems among education policy makers and educators. Opinions on globalization among educated people range from a full acceptance to utter rejection of this concept. For some educators, globalization still remains an unknown and enigmatic notion. Despite divergent viewpoints, globalization being unfolded on earth is a de facto phenomenon.

## GLOBALIZATION AS
## A MULTIFACETED ENTITY

The present-day globalization sweeping the world is a new and specific stage of the overall issue of globalization. The beginning processes of human integration and globalization may coincide with the starting point of human history (Sinagatullin, 2006). In reference to ancient times, the notion of globalization can be applied in its embryonic or archaic meaning, devoid of its digital and nanotechnological content. From global perspectives, human history may be divided into the symbolic eras of:

- migration, integration, and collective activity of various tribes and cultural groups across large geographical areas and continents;
- humanity's regional sociocultural development in the form of city-states and empires (from the Sumerian cities and China to the Glorious Roman Empire);
- global spiritual upsurge owing to the emergence of Christianity and Islam (1st-12th centuries);
- geographical exploration of, and migration to, the non-European part of the world (15th-19th centuries);
- technological revolution and pedagogical renaissance (late 19th-late 20th centuries);
- the rise of digital technology, nanotechnology, and genetic engineering (late 20th-early 21st centuries).

In human history, many progressive breakthroughs have developed side by side with negative tendencies. The growth of religious spirituality has paralleled the waves of barbarism, slavery, and wars. The growth of technology and material luxuries in developed countries has widened the gap between those who possess those luxuries and those who do not.

A third-millennium globalization is characterized by (1) the strengthening of the world economic market, (2) the attempts to organize the global educational space, (3) the emergence of virtual reality and the upsurge of genetic engineering and nanotechnology, (4) the rapid dissemination of the English language throughout the world; (5) the worsening of the ecological situation across the globe; and by (6) the deterioration of children's and teenagers' health. These are just a few major globalizing processes challenging the humankind.

Globalization has brought into the surface unprecedented hazards that threaten human society and require global concern.

# HAZARDS CHALLENGING HUMANITY

*Education as a Slave-Sector of Economy.* Education and science are becoming slave-sectors of economy, something that can be bought and sold, with "knowledge turning into merchandise" (Karpov, 2012). In frantic search of "marketable" majors at colleges and universities, we loose the cultural and humanitarian essence of education, we loose man as a thinking and civilized being. Man is "sold into an economic slavery." What I want to say is that there should be a reasonable share of professional and humanitarian preparation of future specialists, a judicious ratio between preparing an individual for performing a job properly and preparing the individual as a reasoning being and as a whole personality.

*The Clash Between Technology and Tribalism.* In the light of the topic under discussion, Reich's (2000) speculations merit special attention. He prophetically foretold that two great forces would come to the forefront in the 21st century--technology and tribalism. As an opposing force to the growing technological upsurge, tribalism is based on ethnicity, myth, "feelings of solidarity among certain people sharing the same history, language, region, race, customs, or homeland" (p. 34).

Technology cannot be unquestionably positive and tribalism necessarily negative. Technology can ameliorate people's lives and make communication easier; tribalism can deepen people's sense of mutual responsibility. He presaged that technology and tribalism would likely come to a great conflict with each other in this century, which would inevitably be leading to educational polarization and inequities on global and national levels, making a negative impact on children from low income families and those communities who, threatened by the economic and technological globalization, would have to "embrace economic isolation, tribal solidarity, and cultural purity" (p. 34). Reich's prognoses have proved true.

*Surveillance of Human Lives and Their Professional Activities.* Human society is becoming a place where an individual's every step may be recorded. We are witnessing a danger to our privacy and freedom from the relentless increase of surveillance technologies. For instance, while using the Internet, a person may quite unexpectedly run across his name in some of the sites in relation to some theme or data. Our lives are and will be available on the Internet practically forever. Our privacy has been irreversibly cracked. Grant Jeffery (2000) comments this situation as follows:

An undeclared war on personal privacy and freedom is now being waged throughout the world. This war is very real.... Despite the fact that aggressive attacks on our privacy are occurring everyday, the average citizen in the Western world seems unaware of this. One of our most cherished freedoms and human rights--'the freedom to be alone'--is being eroded by the new technological developments and the desire of government to respond to the following threat of terrorism, drug trafficking, and crime. (p. 99)

*Fresh Water Deficits.* Is there abundance of water on our planet? At first glance, water seems to be everywhere and in large quantities; however, of all earth's water, fresh water accounts only for 2.5%. Water is an essential natural resource. This is why it is called blue gold. Water is becoming an expensive commodity, and its deficits are experienced in many corners of the world.

*Energy Shortage.* Energy we use is powered by water, wind, sun, by the burning of biomass (wood), and by nuclear power stations. But most of the energy comes from fossil fuels: oil, natural gas, and coal. Earth's resources of fossil fuels are gradually getting used up. A global decline in oil and gas production may lead to serious socioeconomic crises on the planetary scale with unpredictable outcomes.

*Waste Impact.* Almost everyday I throw away a bag of garbage. So do millions of people across the world. Where does this waste eventually go? It goes to landfills and incinerators. Some of it is recycled. All possible safety measures are unable to save our planet from waste being generated daily by households, various organizations, factories, and plants. Waste makes a negative impact on soil, air, water condition, and on wildlife. It often rots, breeds bacteria, and generates methane gas that contributes to greenhouse effect. If improperly managed, waste becomes a serious health hazard and leads to the spread of infectious and other diseases among children and adults.

## GLOBALIZATION VS. EDUCATION

Globalization makes both positive and negative impact on education. It promotes the integration of national systems of education into one global educational space; fosters positive reorganizations of principles, goals, methods, and content of secondary and higher education; promotes democratic reforms of educational systems; and fosters the ideas of *global education*, which will be the focus of our attention in this section. On the other pole, globalization tends to shatter and destroy the unique and distinctive systems of national education and national culture by introducing Western and other foreign standards of education and child development; promotes the influx of English as a super gigantic foreign language, which ousts other foreign languages from educational and vocational institutions; and decreases the possibilities for children to an equitable and unbiased education. It is the ever-increasing process of globalization that necessitates the design and implementation of global education in secondary schools and other educational institutions.

## THE ESSENCE OF GLOBAL EDUCATION

The nature of global education can be described from at least six angles (Sinagatullin, 2007; 2012). First, global education should be an integral part of general education. In one case, it may look like an add-on program in the form of a theme realized in a series of lessons; in other case, it may occupy larger sections of the teaching/learning process; and still in other case, global education may be infused into the overall tissue of the educational process. Second, it is a new ideology and creed requiring novel modes of thinking towards the monitoring of education and calling for a better understanding of the notions of morality, freedom, and democracy. Third, global education is a concept demanding an unprejudiced worldview and an unbiased attitude to other cultures, alien ways of life, and unaccustomed mentalities. Fourth, it is a progressive and forward-looking movement having emerged from the annals of the present-day globalizing and digital era.

Fifth, global education represents a continuous process whose goals will hardly be realized fully, because the current roaring epoch keeps engendering numerous dilemmas and "headaches" needing an incessant attention and judicious decision. And, sixth, global education appears as a new phase of democratization and humanization of the educational process. All children and adults, despite their ethnic and cultural background, possess a set of common cognitive and physiological needs and drives. All people have the right to live, to be free and happy. Sadly, as humanity has stepped over the threshold of the new millennium, democracy has been eroding and yielding to antidemocratic inclinations in many domains of human activity, including education, a most susceptible entity to societal changes. A crucial goal of global education is strengthening the principles of freedom, democracy, and human rights.

# GLOBAL COMPETENCY

Global education requires that we prepare a favorable educational environment for developing students' global competency, which involves attitudes, a global knowledge base, and skills that they need to productively work and function in a globalizing and interdependent society upon graduation. The notion of *attitude* is most closely related to an individual's modes of thinking, feelings, and readiness to participate in solving international problems and dilemmas facing human society. For example, globally-thinking young men and women should have a clear understanding of the existing global hazards and seek ways to predict, prevent, and combat the dangers through their profession and by other possible means.

*Global knowledge* is an essential component of students' global competency. Contemporary school graduates' global knowledge arsenal is expected to contain the following themes: knowledge on globalization, world history, continents and oceans, world population, nations of the world, health issues, world religions, world languages, energy resources, art and music, cinematography, secondary and higher education across continents, and the global threats to humanity.

A globally competent school graduate is expected to know major facts about the world, about the development of ancient and present-day civilizations and cultures such as Mesopotamia, Egypt, Greece, Rome, Ancient America, the Ottoman Empire, the Russian Empire (prior to 1917), the United States and so forth. The graduate is required to know the contributions of some famous people to the progressive development of human thought, human culture, and world sports: writers Ferenc Molnár (Hungary) and Ernst Junger (Germany); educators Maria Montessori (Italy) and Vitaliy Slastenin (Russia); historians Edward Gibbon and Arnold Toynbee (UK); painters Diego Velásquez (Spain) and Edward Munch (Norway); movie stars Barbara Brilska (Poland) and Ingrid Bergman (Sweden); singers Ella Fitzgerald (U.S.) and Édith Piaf (France); dancer Bob Fosse (U.S.) and premier danseur Rudolf Nureyev (Russia); soccer players Pelé (Brazil) and Diego Maradona (Argentina); and ice hockey players Bobby Hull (Canada) and Boris Mikhaylov (Russia).

Globally minded young people will be amazed to gain knowledge about the natural wonders of the world. Widely considered "wonders" by world travelers during recent centuries are the following breathtaking places (Famighetti, 1999):

- Mt. Everest in the Himalaya mountains, which is the highest peak on earth;
- Victoria Falls, a 343-foot waterfall on the Zambezi River (Africa);
- the Grand Canyon, a stunning steep-walled chasm in Arizona (U.S.);
- Paricutin, one of the world's youngest volcanoes (Mexico);
- the Harbor of Rio de Janeiro (Brazil);
- the Northern Lights, rapidly shifting patches and dancing columns of light of various hues;
- the Great Barrier Reef, a chain of coral reefs in the Coral Sea, off the eastern coast of Queensland (Australia).

I remember seeing the Grand Canyon for the first time.

As soon as the panoramic view of the deep valley below opened to me from the South Rim, I instantaneously fell in love with this greatest hole on earth! What a chasm! Many otherworldly thoughts came to my mind. For instance, it struck me that another planet was opening up in front of me. For millions of years the Colorado River has been carving its way through the formations of the Canyon and is still continuing its unceasing work. Attaining the depth of over a mile, the Grand Canyon is included in the list of the Seven Natural Wonders of the World. The first Europeans to discover the Canyon in 1540 were Spanish explorers. Today the representatives of the Havasupia, Hualapai, Southern Painte, Navajo, and Hopi Indians inhabit the area.

Roaming along the South Rim, I was unable to tear my eyes from the reddish and yellowish "mountains" below. Somewhat below, tourists on horseback were slowly moving downwards along narrow tracks. Several bighorn sheep were luxuriating on a rocky ledge. I thought to myself, "How on earth can these animals manage to inhabit such steep cliffs?" A flock of birds was soaring above, but my "thoughts were soaring below," all along the Colorado-owned valley.

Among the man-created wonders of the world, I recommend educators to see the Moscow Kremlin, a symbol of the Russian State. It houses magnificent treasures, relics, and architectural monuments. The existing towers and walls, built by Italian masters in the late 15th century, constitute 1.4 miles in circumference. When I happen to visit the Kremlin, I like to revisit the Armory and marvel at the 445,170-pound bronze Tsar bell, the largest bell in the world, which stands on a pedestal near the Ivan the Great Bell Tower.

Globally minded students are expected to know that Julius Caesar was a legendary Roman general and statesman, that Boris Pasternak wrote *Doctor Zhivago*, that tea grows in China and Sri Lanka, and that the piranha is an omnivorous freshwater fish inhabiting the South American rivers. But they should also strive to delve into the unknown and poorly discovered enigmas in the world. For the time being, these things are unknown: They are unseen by the naked eye and indecipherable by human brain. Some phenomena considered mystic and bizarre today will inevitably be clarified tomorrow. Today we lack sufficient knowledge and technology to crack these allegedly fantastic phenomena. Formal science usually negates such bizarre knowledge and facts, but genuinely wise and educated people know that this lack of knowledge is only temporary. But it is the knowledge lying on the edge of the rational and irrational that triggers children's curiosities and elicits their motivation to explore the yet-unknown realms.

One of the enigmas on the surface of our planet is the Nazca Desert markings and lines in Peru. They stretch across the plain for about sixty miles and are clearly seen only from a bird's-eye view. From the air one can see a 600-feet-long condor with spread wings, a 600-feet-long monkey, a 150-feet-long spider, a huge parrot, a hummingbird! Scientists claim these colossal drawings were built by ancient people, but the eternal, yet-unsolved questions incessantly linger in people's minds: If so, what did they built them for? Who and what prompted them to create these figures? For instance, Erich von Däniken, who is an advocate of the paleo-contact theory and claims about extraterrestrial influences in ancient times, takes the Nazca Lines as being former airfields for alien spacecraft. Mainstream scientists reject this idea, considering it fantastic and pseudohistoric. Still, who built these huge drawings and lines? Probably the young educated minds of this technological epoch will be able to unravel this riddle.

Now, let us cast a glance into the depths of cosmos. One of the scientific mysteries of our time is dark matter. Astronomers have accepted its existence, which have provided the answer to a range of astronomical phenomena (Blitz, 2011). Astronomers are looking for more clues about how dark matter behaves, and physicists are seeking to detect the particles that compose this stuff.

Another cosmic riddle is the origin of the universe. When and how had all those stars and galaxies come to exist? Had there been any beginning impulse that had contributed to forming these cosmic systems so spectacularly organized? Popular is the big bang theory, which speculates that the universe had been primarily dense and hot until a colossal explosion occurred, and since then, it has been expanding and gradually cooling.

A brand-new theory of the universe is proposed by Teregulov (2006). He takes the universe as being genetic in its essence. All matter in the universe is a rhythm of space and time. Primarily, space and time represent two opposing and disconnected entities, which come into contact when the borderline between them curves and when one opposing side is placed inside the other. Such placement is unfolded in two ways: First, when one polarity is stored inside the other one, and, second, when the second polarity envelopes the first one. These circumstances allow matter to monitor its own steady development within these binary manifestations and to continue molding and shaping a new formation. It is the problem of the balancing and coordinating of space and time that constitutes the essence of the theory of universal genetics. I assume that today's school graduates may add their own clues to this and other cosmic puzzles.

Apart from the puzzles in the realm of the cosmic space-time continuum, there are many enigmas on earth:

- numerous theories on the existence of the legendary Atlantis, which had supposedly been destroyed by a huge cataclysm some 11,600 years ago;
- the monolithic constructions such as the pyramids at Giza, Stonehenge, and the sites at Baalbeck;
- references to vimanas (flying machines) in the ancient epics of India;
- speculations about the origin of man. Some theorists claim that reasoning life could have been brought by aliens from the outer space;
- references to the facts that humans could have lived alongside dinosaurs;
- hypotheses supporting the possibility of traveling through space at a speed much faster than that of light.

Contemporary school graduates with a global perspective in mind should possess corresponding *skills* to productively interact in a globalizing and interdependent society. They are required to be able to communicate in one of world languages such as English, Spanish, German, French, Russian, Chinese, or Arabic. To adequately communicate in a global sociocultural space, one needs to possess at least the skills of oral speech in a world language. But the ideal form of possessing a language is the ability to possess all four groups of skills: listening with comprehension, speaking, reading, and writing. Among other international languages, English is the most distributed and systematically used language across the world. It is lingua franca No.1, with other "smaller" lingua francas centralized on particular regions: Spanish--in Latin America, German--in Central Europe, and Russian--in the post-Soviet sociolinguistic space.

Graduates should possess skills of interacting with people from various cultural and religious backgrounds. A good method of developing such skills is organizing a variety of student exchange and international travel programs. International experiences tremendously enhance students' multicultural and global scope, help them become less ethnocentric, and teach them to view their own culture and country from different viewpoints.

## GLOBAL CURRICULUM

One of the basic prerequisites of global education is the following: All students, despite their ethnic, racial, gender, language, and social class backgrounds, should possess a global competency--attitude, knowledge base, and skills--that they require to productively function in a globalizing and interdependent world. Our human race represents fundamentally one flock, with vital human needs across the continents and seas being practically the same. As it is so, all schools throughout the world are expected to have similar requirements for the global part of the school curriculum and, probably, similar textbooks on some of the subject areas. In understanding the world, we encounter the same laws of physics, chemistry, the same mathematical formulas, the same rules of phonetics, grammar and stylistics if we learn one and the same foreign language. For every school student across the world, the names of the countries and their capitals will stay the same. So will the names of the oceans, seas, rivers, lakes, mountain chains, and summits. The recorded history of humanity will likely be the same too.

Consequently, a salient part of a school curriculum, virtually in all the nation states, may reflect the same material. We may call it the *global component of the school curriculum*. Not a single child and adolescent should be deprived of this important component, because, at large part, each one child is a precious individual for our multicultural and multilingual world. This part of the curriculum should not be politically, religiously, or ideologically motivated. Students should be allowed to judiciously analyze and provide their own viewpoints about any country, any system of ideas or principles, and any personality.

In reality, textbooks and other materials used in schools and colleges seem to contain, with different degrees of inclusion, global, federal and local components. For instance, all school students across the world study mathematics, the fundamentals of which are virtually the same for all learners. Likewise they learn physics, chemistry, zoology, world geography, world history as well as other disciplines that incorporate the humanitarian issues pertaining to all humanity. However, there is a lot of ethnic and cultural bias and prejudice in designing and implementing educational programs in different cultures. Unequal access to global knowledge, universal values, and information (that is important for each learner of the entire globe) is a major causal factor of the educational inequality and inequity being currently experienced throughout the world.

This global component in school curricula on the planetary level may include the basic knowledge and skills indispensable for all students who would become citizens of their own country and of the world. What a brilliant curriculum it would have been if we had similar textbooks on the sciences in the secondary schools of all countries! Likewise, similar textbooks on the humanities! Such an educational reform would have significantly promoted a path to an unbiased and non-marginalized education.

Drawing from the issues presented above, I urge educators to capitalize on developing students' global competency and literacy, as the following ideas suggest:

## Enhance Students' Global Competency through the Social Studies Curriculum

Promote learners' global competency while instructing history, geography, sociology, world cultures, and other subjects included into social studies. Convey to them the knowledge about the major global events in world history, such as, for example, the emergence of Buddhism ($5^{th}$ century B.C.), Christianity ($1^{st}$ century A.D.), and Islam ($7^{th}$ century A.D.); the opening of the Americas (1492); the creation of the first photograph (1827); the spreading of the European languages (15th-19th centuries); the discovery of penicillin (1928); the invention of telephone (1876) and radio (1900); the breakthrough into space (1957); the women's liberation movement (1960s-1970s); Beatlemania (1970s); Macdonaldization (1960s-present); and the arrival of the digital era (1990s-present).

Recommend not only widely known knowledge about the world but also facts and information that may be little known or unknown to students and public at large. Organize the knowledge construction process by optimally navigating between the basic knowledge recommended by the program and knowledge available through the digital and ordinary mass media. Present knowledge by clustering it within certain topics.

## Use Science Courses and Mathematics to Enhance Students' Global Competency

Earth science, biology, chemistry, physics, and mathematics with its branches are highly international disciplines. They are taught in every country. The essence of these subject areas are truly universal, although we understand that certain material in textbooks and related manuals must respond to local economic and sociocultural conditions.

Ignite students' curiosities by indicating the importance of science courses for solving vital problems in the world. For example, if you teach at a San Francisco school, you may remind students of the 1906 earthquake that had destroyed much of the city, analyze the nature of earthquakes in other parts of the world, and propose constructive recommendations to combat this hazard. When touching upon the issue of electricity, remind students of the Hoover Dam on the Colorado River, producing hydroelectric power, and of other dams bridging other rivers in the world. Meriting attention is the Ataturk Dam on the Euphrates River; it generates electricity, and its water reservoir irrigates the nearby land, thus increasing the production of cotton.

## Introduce Students to the Contemporary World Cultures and Civilizations

Different approaches have been provided by historians to classify civilizations. For example, the English historian Arnold Joseph Toynbee divided history into 21 developed and 5 "arrested" civilizations. Utkin (2001) provides the contours of seven civilizations. Stemming from the previous research on the topic and adding a little bit of my personal conjecture, the contemporary human world can symbolically be subdivided into at least eight groups of huge and discernible cultures (Sinagatullin, 2006).

1. Atlantic civilization, including the countries of Western Europe (excluding the Scandinavian countries and Denmark), Canada, the United States, Australia, New Zealand, and the Baltic states--Estonia, Latvia and Lithuania;

2. Nordic civilization, to which belong Norway, Sweden, Denmark, and Iceland;

3. Eurasian civilization, extending from Poland, Czech Republic, and Bulgaria to Mongolia and the eastern borders of Russia and from the northern fringes of Russia and Finland to Turkmenistan;

4. Middle-Eastern civilization, stretching from Turkey to Pakistan and from Iran to Yemen, including the Islamic countries of northern Africa

5. South and East Asian civilization, from India to Japan and from China to Indonesia and the Philippines;

6. Pacific civilization, the boundaries of which extend from Northern Mariana Islands to Tonga and Fiji and from Palau to French Polynesia;

7. African civilization, spreading all over the Sub-Saharan Africa, including Madagascar;

8. Latin American civilization, extending all over South America, including the Caribbean and Mexico.


## Promote Student Exchange

Help organize student partnerships and exchanges with schools in other countries so that your students might travel and deepen their global scope and master foreign language skills in real-life situations. Students participating in such programs gain global knowledge and skills of interaction with people from various cultural backgrounds and bring back valuable memories. Such experiences increase their multicultural and intercultural experience, experiential knowledge base, and they become more tolerant toward alien cultures, other ways of life, and unaccustomed mentality.


## Help Organize Internships

Assist students in finding international internships. Some universities, colleges, and internationally oriented organizations, both in your country and abroad, may offer internship programs for high school students during their summer vacations. Internships help students get acquainted with a new culture and new modes of labor activity, create a network of contacts, and gain an understanding of the growing global interconnectedness. Assuredly, internships provide students with opportunities for practicing and mastering foreign language skills.

And lastly, ensure students' understanding of the fact that this planet, beautifully rotating around the sun, is eventually their larger residence. With all its waters, lands, fauna and flora, it belongs to them, but only for a lifespan; therefore each young girl and young boy must be proud of having been given the opportunity to live on this planet. Each young graduate must strive to be as useful as possible to humanity.

Capitalize on developing reflective and creative citizens of the world, capable of making wise decisions and taking responsibility for the present and future of their home country and the world. Let each school graduate remember, once in a while, the above quote from Socrates. Let this insightful phrase remind us that this planet, which is only formally divided by borders, is our common home and haven.

We live in human society that is not deprived of evil and corruption. Should educational institutions prepare passive survivors and consumers or active reorganizers and refiners of this society? The next chapter examines these and some other points.

*Chapter 15*

# EQUATING SCHOOL WITH HUMAN SOCIETY

*Education is the most powerful weapon which you can use to change the world.*
Nelson Mandela

*You must be the change you wish to see in the world.*
Mahatma Gandhi

Millions of times in my pedagogical career I have heard the motto calling educators and parents to prepare a child for life. At first glance, there is nothing wrong in this slogan. In fact, preparing a child for life is one of the objectives of any educational institution; and it is a prime goal of parents. Only one salient question hangs in the air still unanswered: For what sort of life should we prepare young girls and boys? For the one that *we see right now* looking out of the window or the life that we see after switching on the TV set or for the life that *should be*? Or the one that we are building together with children on a daily basis in the classroom?

Let us remember what a priest says in his summons. Does he say "People, behave as all the people do"? Not at all! He continually calls people to behave decently. The admonitions the priest proposes are realized only by a definite number of individuals in a given community or society. The priest calls the congregation members to build a new life based on godly rules. When more individuals change their attitudes to life, to their families, their ways of interaction with a neighbor, and change their understanding of why and for what man has been born, the nearest community and the wider society will undoubtedly change for the better.

Let us remember what a doctor recommends a patient. Does the doctor say "Please, Mr. Brown, live on as you yourself and all the rest of the people in our society have been living and your health will improve"? In addition to recommending the required medication, a prudent doctor will inevitably call his patient to pursue a definite diet and to change lifestyles. If many people with physical or mental health troubles change their diet, ways of life, and their attitudes to the people surrounding them, the immediate community and the wider society will change accordingly as well.

Let us remember what a builder may say to a person who invites the builder to reconstruct the old-fashioned house that has only a few modern conveniences. The builder will likely suggest building a new house that will be convenient, modern, and look towards the future, a house where this person and his family members will feel comfortable and happy. A wise and professionally minded builder or engineer will propose a design unlike other less convenient houses. A range of houses like this will likely change the local community and local architectural infrastructure for the better by adding a touch of socioeconomic convenience and aesthetic form.

## FROM SCHOOL TO THE OUTER SOCIETY

School should not only be a life itself, but a *new life* in itself, a life that engenders young graduates who are eager to contribute fresh sparks of creativity in the enhancement of the entire society. School should contain an idea of how to change a society for the better and be a place where this idea is generated and implemented. School is required to show others, with the help of secular principles, how to use children's educational competencies and moral attitude for ameliorating the welfare of humanity. School graduates should be prepared as carriers of new ways of peaceful coexistence on planet earth. Upon graduation, they should know how to prevent, overcome, and eradicate social, economic, and intercultural mistakes and sins committed by previous generations.

Preparing children for life also sounds good. They should know the material world; they must adapt themselves to a given society; they are obliged to raise families; they need to be good citizens of their own country and the world; and they should not violate criminal, labor, and civic codes. But school graduates should not be prepared only for a life that is, but they themselves should build a better life in school and "take this life out of the school premises" upon graduation.

Graduates should build a better life based on both the positive arsenal having already been garnered by humanity and on novel ideas required by the current era. A school is a social institution only to such an extent when it encompasses human society's *positive sides*. It should promote children's development in the rightful direction. There is also the other side in human society that is packed with sinful activities such as drug and alcohol addiction, prostitution, adultery, child and woman abuse, and corruption. Therefore we loathe using the phase "It is necessary to prepare a child for life." Not all that we call *social life* should be internalized and become an "individual property" of a child. There are *negative sides* in human society, which should not come out as models for internalization and further imitation.

I often compare an unborn baby's nine-month development in the womb to his development for 18 years after his birth. In the first case, the mother "prepares" the child for the world by nurturing the unborn creature with all her physiological strength. She takes tender care of her seed. In the second case, as soon as a he or a she "sees the world," the things change. The newly born baby becomes a lawful offspring of the mother and the father and, at the same time and immediately, becomes a tiny social being, even though the baby has not yet stepped into the trail of socialization. Despite this fact, various institutionalized structures "start taking care of the child." The more the child grows in age and matures, the greater the number of external structures that get into contact with him.

In the first case, the mother is always "present" with the not-yet-born fetus. Even a hungry mother can provide for her child developing under her heart. In the second case, as the child grows, he or she becomes more and more isolated from the family circle. The young adult adapts to the society and exerts more effort to live as other people do and to imitate both good and bad sides of the society. The school and parents help the child considerably to become a social being, i.e. to live as other people do. The school, parents, other people surrounding the child, and all the plethora of socioeconomic and cultural institutions push hard to equate the child's attitude, capabilities, and heart with the existing society and its explicit and implicit laws. This child, who is not to blame for his coming into being, has every right to be taken care of on a maximal level of love and attention. But it is during this 18-year period that parents, school, and society "start losing hold of the child."

I appreciate the greatest ideas and creeds of numerous theorists and educators who emphasize the importance of society and socialization in promoting children's and adolescents' cognitive and personality development. At the same time I permit myself to challenge these ideas. Human society is currently undergoing dramatic changes accompanied by startling crises.

Undoubtedly, education is a process of living and schools and colleges should represent and be oriented to present life, should be part of our society; but they should also function ahead of time, become holy institutions from a pedagogical perspective, be reservoirs of all prior wisdom and fundamental knowledge, and present examples of decent and righteous conduct. I agree that a school is a part of society and embodies social life, but it should be the *best part* of society and symbolize this best part.

At the rise of the 20th century, educators believed that schools should take up and continue the traditions and activities with which children are already familiar in their interactions with parents and extended family members. However, homes and communities have changed since the early 20th century. Especially noticeable within the previous 40 to 50 years are family divorces, family quarrels, alcoholism, the striving to material values, and child abuse. The monogamic family has become a "thin" and "crumbly" social institution, especially in the northern hemisphere.

In this, globalizing and harsh epoch, the child should not only bring to school positive sides and manners of good behavior from family and community, but, also and primarily, bring good manners, wisdom, and knowledge from the school to his family and society, like a believer brings sacred thoughts out a religious shrine.

We purportedly expect that our school children should internalize the existing societal norms and be good citizens of their countries and the world. We prepare them for life and work in the present-day human world. We educate them and say "Be a good citizen!" But for what kind of the outer society are we preparing them? Let's have a brief glimpse at what is expecting a newly-baked school graduate in our 21st-century world.

## THE WORLD EXPERIENCES NUMEROUS CRISES

Parallel to the so-called "harmonious development," the world we all live in is in a constant process of crises elicited by a whole range of factors.

*Sociopolitical Crisis.* Contemporary times are characterized by the struggle between the forces of democracy and authoritarianism and by the existence of the huge contradiction between the movements of globalists and anti-globalists. Another contradiction being unfolded is between endeavors of people for privacy and freedom and the increasing surveillance on the part of the state, government and related institutions.

*Demographic Crisis.* The world population is expected to reach 9.5 billion by 2050, with 90% of the population increase coming from developing countries. An increasing population growth is estimated in Jordan, Mali, Niger, Yemen, Pakistan, Libya, Algeria, Cambodia, Mexico, Egypt, India, Bangladesh, Iran, Brazil, and Turkey. In 2050 the population of Africa may rise 2,3 fold; of Asia, Latin America, and Oceania, 1,5 fold. The population of industrialized countries will be decreasing, especially in Europe and Japan. By 2050 the population in Europe will likely decrease by 14% and in Japan, by 17% (Rimashevskaya, 2002a; 2002b). Overpopulation may become a major factor accelerating poverty and unemployment in families and problems in educational institutions.

*Ecological Crisis.* There is every reason to believe that humanity is on the brink of an environmental catastrophe. The increasing air pollution results in acid rain, global warming, and the destruction of the ozone layer. Deforestation disrupts the formation of rain. The pollution of air, water, and land destroys the natural habitats of plants and animals.

*Economical Crisis.* The division of the world into the rich minority and poor majority is increasing rapidly. By 2050 the population of southern countries may increase dramatically (Utkin, 2001). Poor families will hardly be able to provide all their children with quality education. Malnutrition, juvenile delinquency, and school dropouts are likely to rise. In reflecting on economical issues, I remembered a dinner-table chat having once taken place in our house when I was a high-school student.

> There were four people at the table: my parents, myself, and my father's sister. We all had gone through various serious and trivial topics and my father, in keeping with a previous theme, said that humanity had been facing a range of challenges such as flu epidemics and heart diseases. His sister, then aged 55, nodded as if agreeing with him and added: "Yes, it is exactly so, but folks, among all the calamities people encounter, hunger must be the worst one."
>
> Deeply imbedded in my consciousness, this phrase, since then, has often been springing up in my mind. Not in vain did my father's sister mention the notion of hunger in that social context. She herself had experienced the economically difficult years after World War II when there had been scanty food in the village. Under such circumstances survival had been at stake. Apparently, she had not been the only person who had experienced economic hardships.

In recorded history an abject and unbearable hunger tends to have common consequences. People may resort to eating wild animals, even rats and mice, grass, straw, and some may even turn to cannibalism. It is sad to acknowledge that each year thousands of people on earth die of hunger, including young children and teenagers. Strangely enough, on the other pole, thousands of affluent people sit at appetizingly laid out tables, select the best slices of chicken and fish, and cheerfully discuss how to team their salads and meat courses with an appropriate wine. There is a prudent proverb reportedly originated on the Asian continent and which is worth considering: "If you see in any one place a table richly covered with meals, there inevitably exists, in some other place and at this very time, another table with no meals on it."

*Anthropological Crisis.* This crisis stems from the neglect of fundamental human values, laws, and etiquettes of decent social and professional behavior. Extremely destructive in nature is *corruption*, which shatters the moral and juridical foundations of citizenship and destroys the progressive development of humanity. Noticeable across the world is people's striving for *materialistic assets* to the detriment of spiritual values such as empathy, honesty, civic virtues, and altruism. Young people have become egocentric and devoted to money. Their devotion to the Internet and cell phones knows no borders.

One of the most disastrous forms of crisis is *war*. Throughout human history the world has endured 13 years of war for every single year in peace. Since the end of WWII, the number of wars and conflicts has increased tremendously (Jeffrey, 2000). Military conflicts and wars lead to human casualties and to the destruction of property and resources. War has an incomparably disastrous impact on education. The Greek tragedian Sophocles said that "war loves to seek its victims in the young." By this he might have meant not only the young soldiers who die during wars but also young civilians who fall victims of the effects of war and suffer its consequences.

I am always surprised at the fact why humans--who are reasoning beings and possess tremendous intellectual abilities--engage in military conflicts and wars. Why do they engage in such organized and well-planned fights against each other? Astonishingly, armed conflicts continue to erupt and there seems to be no stopping them.

In the animal world, the species tend to engage only into single combats, mostly for winning the sympathies of female partners. But one surprising evidence exists in the world of ants. In passing, I would like to briefly focus on this incredible miracle. Mark Moffett (2011) assures us that battles among arts can be similar to human military fights, despite striking differences between humans and ants in terms of biology and societal structure. Normally, ant colonies consist of females functioning as workers or soldiers, occasionally a few males serving as drones, and one or more fertile queens. Even though ant colonies are decentralized and workers know little about making combat decisions, that, nevertheless, proves effective at the group level. This process is called "swam intelligence." Even though ants and humans beings have divergent styles of life, "they fight their foes for many of the same economic reasons, including access to dwelling spaces, territory, food and even labor-- certain ant species kidnap competitors to serve as slaves" (p. 66). Moffett further writes that:

> The most breathtaking example of colony allegiance in the ant world is that of the *Linepithema humile* ant. Though native to Argentina, it has spread to many other parts of the world by hitching rides in human cargo. In California the biggest of these 'supercolonies' ranges from San Francisco to the Mexican border and may contain a trillion individuals, united throughout by the same 'national' identity. Each month millions of Argentine ants die along battlefields that extend for miles around San Diego, where clashes occur with three other colonies in wars that may have been going on since the species arrived in the state a century ago... The violent expansions of ant supercolonies bring to mind how human colonial superpowers once eradicated smaller groups, from Native Americans to Australian Aborigines. Luckily, ...our allegiances can shift over time to let immigrants in, to permit nations to fluidly define themselves. (p. 69)

It may well happen that scientists studying animal behavior will discover an evidence of collective warfare among some other species. For us, not this is important. We, peace-loving human beings, must seek collective efforts within the *human world* to combat those forces who strive to wage military actions.

All the above-mentioned negative and critical states of affairs are closely intertwined, and, in most cases, it is man who triggers such crises. The rejuvenation of intimate relations between the sexes reaching down to middle school students, the growth of STDs, prostitution involving school- and college-age students, and the unprecedented adultery occurring in a considerable number of families are all striking manifestations of our society's moral decline. Consequently, the overall crisis unfolding these days on the surface of planet earth is anthropological in its very essence and roots. These and other degrading and deteriorating processes stem from human sins i.e. from the incapability or unwillingness to manage and monitor one's vital needs and emotions.

In these unfolding circumstances, other similar questions arise: Should we prepare children for this life by developing their survival skills to adjust and adapt to the existing circumstances and existing crises or should we develop our students as individuals who might work to prevent these negative processes and create a new human civilization devoid of corruption and confrontations? I myself would have voted for the latter.

I continue this section with thoughts about what educators can do to make the school a better place for children's development as individuals and social beings.

## Foster Children's Inner Potential

Regardless of ethnic, cultural, gender, language, and social class backgrounds and irrespective of behavioral, physical, mental, and socioemotional characteristics, each child possesses inner and, often, latent capabilities that we should unravel, diagnose, recognize, and develop. Each child has his or her *cognitive potential* involving progressive changes in the individual's intelligence, language, and thought; *physical potential* that can be developed and used for the good of humanity; and *socioemotional potential* involving progressive changes in the individual's relationships with the surrounding people as well as involving changes in personality. Each child possesses an invaluable *creative potential* for some particular activities; *social potential*, a craving for ameliorating life and human society for the better; and *humanitarian potential*, an inner craving for helping people in need.

## Teach Students to Change the World for the Better

Provide extra efforts to prepare students not only for the life that is unfolding outside the school premises, but also and primarily, for a *life to be*. For you and for me, for all educators and teacher educators, all parents, all relatives, all sisters and brothers, all grandparents, and for all people involved in educating children, it becomes a matter of principal importance to prepare children and adolescents for changing the world for the better.

The graduates who receive school certificates and university diplomas should be prepared to combat human sins and social ills such as ethnocentrism and racism; corruption and prostitution; tobacco smoking; drug and alcohol abuse; juvenile delinquency and teenage pregnancy; domestic violence; child abuse; religious confrontations; arms race, military conflicts, and wars; and poverty. The new generation of young people is required to build a life based on principles of empathy; honesty; mutual help; respect for the elderly, parents, and the teacher; and love for the neighbor.

## Help Children Build a New Human Society

I often look at the map of the world in my study. I see that this large home of ours is on its proper place in the solar system and in the Milky Way. But something is wrong with it, not with the world of fauna and flora, but with the human world. The animal species--marine and land mammals, fishes, birds, and insects--live in harmony but, at the same time, they struggle for survival. Attacking and eating one another is a natural means of survival in their habitats. They eat to live, and they eat smaller and weaker species. Some of the animal species are vegetarians. Nevertheless, they "know" accepted standards of behavior and certain norms that should not be exceeded.

When one leads a horse to a watering-place, the horse will drink only the needed quantity of water without exceeding what is essential for that horse's needs. A lion, after strangling a roe deer, will consume only the required amount of prey that is essential to stave off hunger. It seems the lion knows about the existence of other lions and other species who also want a little bit of their share predetermined for them by the natural laws of nature. Even though animals ferociously struggle for survival, they tend not to overstep the existing norms in eating, drinking, and behavior. What about human species? The overwhelming majority of human beings eat, drink, and behave to excess without taking into account the required norms and rules. Although human beings tend or at least want to live in harmony and peace, they often overdo in satisfying their vital needs.

In some of its features, the contemporary human world is more likely to resemble that of the animal world. Many people struggle for survival because they lack food, lack love, have no shelter, and have no jobs. They overcome hardships to make ends meet. Other people also "struggle to continue to live and exist" but by different means: by stealing, money laundering, exploiting other people's labor, and by producing and selling drugs. A question arises: Should the human world resemble that of the animal world? In some ways it should because we, humans, are a part of nature. But the human world should be based on higher values, civilized and humanistic principles, laws, and norms, not merely on survival skills.

What I am driving at is the following: If we prepare a child for a life that *is*, then we have to develop, along with other skills and abilities, students' survival skills and survival competency. But if we want to prepare graduates for a *life to be*, then our obligation is to educate them so as to develop their abilities and skills not only to overcome the existing difficulties but to change the world for the better and simultaneously to become good members of their home countries and the world. Cleaning and purifying the world from human sins and human dirt becomes a task of prime concern for contemporary graduates. *It is now high time to educate a new social being for building a new society. New graduates must build a new world.*

## Be Prepared Yourself!

In promoting students' inner and social potential to change the world for the better, you yourself must be prepared to contribute to the amelioration of human society and to save if from further calamites. It is only when the teacher knows how to do it that he or she will be able to teach children to realize this same goal. "The world of fauna and the world of flora need to be protected, saved, and sustained. The human world needs to be improved. Let us undertake concrete efforts and measures to turn our entire planet into a better place to live, to work and, to realize our best plans" (Sinagatullin, 2009b, p. 224).

Ending this chapter, I again want to stress this important point: One of the mistakes of pedagogy is that educators tend to educate a child for the life and society existing outside the homes and educational institutions, thus making school equal with contemporary societal norms. Instead, educators have to prepare a graduate who is inspired with novel ambitions and enthusiasm for building a new society based on truly humanistic and civilized canons and principles. A school itself must represent such a society in its primary and smaller form.

# CONCLUSION

Teaching young people is one of the most important and noble professions a person can have. Most of the work teachers perform often has a long-lasting impact upon their disciples. Educators have a great responsibility for those they teach and are responsible and answerable for the entire human society.

In contemporary society a considerable number of people smoke, drink alcoholic beverages to excess, take narcotics, engage in corruption, commit adultery, homicide, cause the destruction of the ecosystem, give false testimony, engage in war and terrorism, and exploit women and children. Schools should teach children and adolescents to keep away from alcohol, drugs, and tobacco smoking; avoid corruption in all its forms; love the neighbor; preserve and protect fauna and flora; be honest and tolerant; combat attempts of people to start a military conflict or war; and treat women, the elderly, and children with loving compassion.

A school is a place where a child and later, an adolescent, should learn not only to live as other people in society do but to live a better life, be a carrier of novel ideas, and be a prototype for an ideal social being. A school is a part of society, but it must be the cradle of a new, even more wholesome society, a model to be imitated. Teachers should not say, "Hey, boys and girls, contemporary world is harsh, therefore you must be prepared to be tough, sharp-witted, crafty, and ambitious and opportunistic." Teachers must persuade and prepare their disciples to be good members of human society, to multiply the positive sides and combat the negative sides of life, and to refine and change the world for the better. In so doing, schools need to work hand in hand with parents and various educational and social structures.

A true educator always gives up some of herself or himself and pays for the pleasure of working with the young. An educator sows seeds that, upon falling on a field, give birth to dozens of other, strong young seedlings.

We are all merely guests on this planet. Let us act in noble ways. Let us treat our own and other people's children benevolently and develop in the young positive and tolerant attitude to, and concern for, all that exists on our planet earth. This new centennial is signaling us to hurry to solve pressing problems facing education before it is late. Time passes fast and the future will soon be upon us.

Delivering these notes to the curious and open minded reader, I have not resolved in any final way the many problems facing education. I have addressed only some specific issues and problems and, I hope, have provoked thought and raised awareness of challenges facing teachers and all those who are involved in educating the young. If any of the ideas in this publication have inspired readers to further contemplate ways to ameliorate the educational and child-rearing processes, then I will consider that my efforts have succeeded.

# REFERENCES

Akhiyarov, K. S. (2000). *Narodnaya pedagogika i sovremennaya shkola* [Folk pedagogy and the contemporary school]. Ufa, Russia: Bashkir State Pedagogical University.

Alexandre Dumas. (2012). *Wikipedia.* Retrieved from http://en. wikipedia.org/wiki/alexandre_Dumas

Banks, J. A. (2004). Teaching for social justice, diversity, and citizenship in a global world. *The Educational Forum, 68*(4), 296-305.

Banks, J. A. (2009). Human rights, diversity, and citizenship education. *The Educational Forum, 73*(2), 100-110.

Barr, G. (1995). *Meeting the global challenges to eliminate poverty.* Retrieved from http://incommon.web.ca/anglais/about/mission.html.

Batmanghelidj, F. (1995). *Your body's many cries for water: You are not sick, you are thirsty! Don't treat thirst with medications!* Falls Church, V.A.: Global Health Solutions.

Bim-Bad, B. M. (2002). *Pedagogicheskiy entsiklopedicheskiy slovar* [Pegagogical encyclopedic dictionary]. Moscow: Bolshaya Rossiyskaya Entsiklopediya.

Biography. (2012). *Hamilton Arts.* Retrieved from http://www. virginiahamilton.com/biography/

Blitz, L. (2011). The dark side of the Milky Way. *Scientific American, 305*(4), 22-29.

Boroditsky, L. (2011). How language shapes thought. *Scientific American, 304*(2), 43-45.

Carter, R. (1999). Mental health: A challenge for the new century. In R. Farmighetti (Ed.), *The world almanac and book of facts 2000* (p. 41). Mahwah, NJ: World Almanac Books.

Comenius, J. A. (2009). *Wikipedia.* Retrieved from http://en.wikipedia. org/wiki/Comenius

Crystal, D. (1997). *English as a global language.* Cambridge, UK. Cambridge University Press.

Dewey, J. (1897). My pedagogic creed. *The School Journal, LIV (3).* Retrieved from http://222.infed.org/archives/e-dew-pc.htm

Ermolaev, V. (1991). Budet dzit shkola--budet dzit selo [If the school exists, so will the village]. *Narodnoye Obrazovaniye, 8,* 14-19.

Famighetti, R. (Ed.). (1999). *The world almanac and book of facts, 2000.* Mahwah, N.J.: World Almanac Books.

Felder, R. M., & Henriques, E. R. (1995). Learning and teaching styles in foreign and second language education. *Foreign Language Annals, 28*(1), 21-31.

Fuller, W. E. (1982). *The old country school.* Chicago, IL: University of Chicago Press.

Gabucci, A. (Ed.). (2005). *Rome.* Berkeley, CA: University of California Press.

Gold, Y. (1984). Burnout: A major problem for the teaching profession. *Education, 104*(3), 271-274.

*Going global: Preparing our students for an interconnected world.* (2009). San Francisco, CA: Asia Society.

Greatest needs: Rural education in China. (2011). *Give2asia.* Retrieved from http://give2asia.org/greatestneeds-ruraleducation-china

Huston J. (1989). Teacher burnout and effectiveness: A Case Study. *Education, 110*(1), 70-78.

Italian language. (2011). *Wikipedia.* Retrieved from http://www.wikipedia. org/wiki/Italian_language

Janssen, S. (Ed.). (2011). *The world almanac and book of facts 2011.* New York, NY: World Almanac Books.

Jeffrey, G. R. (2000). *Surveillance society: The rise of Antichrist.* Toronto, Canada: Frontier Research Publications.

Jordan, R. (1975). Effects of children's physical attractiveness on teachers' evaluations. *Journal of Educational Psychology, 67*(5), 599-609.

Karpov, A. O. (2012). Kommodifikatsiya obrazovaniya [The commoditization of education]. *Pedagogika, 2,* 3-12.

Kiplangat, C. (2003, February 24). *Our languages are dying.* Retrieved from http://www.globalpolicy.org/globaliz/cultural/2003/0224language.htm

Kudriavaya, N. V. (1993). *Lev Tolstoy o smisle dzizni* [Leo Tolstoy on the essence of life]. Moscow: Krasniy Proletariy.

Lado, R. (1964). *Linguistics across cultures. Applied linguistics for language teachers.* Ann Arbor, MI: The University of Michigan Press.

Laskey, J. (2008). *The health benefits of water.* Retrieved from http://www.everyday/health.com/water-health/water-body-health.aspx

Lawless, L. K. (2012). *What is French? Facts and figures about the French language.* Retrieved from http://www.about.com/od/francophonie/ss/whatisfrench_2htm

*Learning Spanish in Spain and Latin America.* (2006). Salamanca, Spain: Don Quijote

Maher, F., & Tetreault, M. K. (1999). *Knowledge versus pedagogy: The marginalization of teacher education.* Retrieved from http://findarticles.com/p/articles/mi_ga3860/is_199901/ai_n8828789/

Mango, C. (2005). *Byzantium: The Empire of the New Rome.* London: Phoenix.

Maslach, C., & Jackson, S. E. (1981). The measurement of experienced burnout. *Journal of Occupational Behavior, 2,* 99-113.

McKenna, M. (2011). The enemy within. *Scientific American, 304*(4), 26-33.

McPherson, R. B. (1983). Teacher dignity: An antidote to burnout. *Education, 104*(2), 199-203.

Miss Universe. (2011). *Wikipedia.* Retrieved from http://en/wikipedia.org/wiki/Miss_Universe

Moffett, M. W. (2011). Ants and the art of war. *Scientific American, 305*(6), 64-69.

Nasser, N. (2008). U.S. Hispanic population to triple by 2050. *USA Today.* Retrieved from http://www.usatoday,com

Native voices: Authors. (2011). *Learner.* Retrieved from http://www.learner.org/amerpass/unit01/authors-6.html

Occupational safety and health. (2011). *Wikipedia.* Retrieved from http://en.wikipedia.org/wki/Occupational_safety_and_health

Orey, C. (2009). *Olive oil: A complete guide to nature's liquid gold.* New York, NY: Kensington Books.

Ortiz, S. J. (1992). *Woven stone.* Tucson, AZ: The University of Arizona Press.

Oswald, P., & Schulz-Benesch, G. (Ed.). (1997). *Basic ideas of Montessori's educational theory.* Retrieved from http://www.moteaco.com/abcclio/basic/html

Parker, M., St. John. (2007). *William Shakespeare.* Andover, UK: Pitkin Publishing.

Physical attractiveness. (2012). *Wikipedia.* Retrieved from en.wikipedia. org/wiki/Physical_attractiveness.

Piskunov, A. I. (Ed.). (2005). *Istoriya pedagogiki i obrazovaniya* [The history of pedagogy and education]. Moscow: TT Sfera.

Pollets, D. (2008). Internet sex addiction: Case studies and treatment. *Psychology Today.* Retrieved from http://www.psychologytoday. com/blog/mindful-sex/200808/internet-sex-addiction-ca...

Rapogov, V. G. (Ed.). (2004). Mirovaya entsiklopediya biogrfiy [The world encyclopedia of biographies] (Vol. 4). Moscow: Mir Knigi.

Reich, R. B. (2000). The two great forces of the future. In R. Famighetti (Ed.), *The world almanac and book of facts, 2000* (pp. 33-34). Mahwah, NJ: World Almanac Books.

Religious education. (2012). *Wikipedia.* Retrieved from http://en. wikipedia.org/wiki/Religious_education

Review of rural education in India. (2011). *JustIndianSchools.* Retrieved from http://www.justindianschools.com/articles/108-review-of-rural-education-in-india.html

Richman, L. C. (1978). The effects of facial disfigurement on teachers' perception of ability in cleft palate children. *Cleft Palate Journal 15*(2). Retrieved from http://digital.library.pitt.edu/c/cleftpalate/pdf/e20986v15n2.10.pdf

Rimashevskaya, N. M. (2002a). Naseleniye v rakurse globalizatsii [Population in the light of globalization]. In N. M. Rimashevskaya, V. F. Galetsky, & A. A. Ovsiannikov (Eds.), *Naseleniye i globalizatsiya* (pp. 8-28). Moscow: Nauka.

Rimashevskaya, N. M. (2002b). Demograficheskiye problemi globalizatsii [The demographic problems of globalization]. In N. M. Rimashevskaya, V. F. Galetsky, & A. A. Ovsiannikov (Eds.), *Naseleniye i globalizatsiya* (pp. 173-227). Moscow: Nauka.

Robert Louis Stevenson. (2012). *Wikipedia.* Retrieved from http://en. wikipedia.org/ wiki/Robert_Louis_Stevenson

Santrock, J. W. (2002). *Life-span development* (8th ed.). New York, NY: McGraw-Hill.

Sinagatullin, I. M. (2002). Russia on the horizon: The role, means and factors of folk pedagogy in educating children. *Current Politics and Economics of Russia, Eastern and Central Europe, 17*(2), 113-126.

Sinagatullin, I. M. (2006). *The impact of globalization on education.* New York, NY: Nova Science Publishers.

Sinagatullin, I. M. (2007). Global education: A glance at the Russian front. *International Journal of Educational Reform, 16*(20, 128-138.

Sinagatullin, I. M. (2009a). A triumphant global crusade of contemporary era: The impact of the English language on education. *International Journal of Educational reform, 18*(4), 300-310.

Sinagatullin, I. M. (2009b). *Teaching is more than pedagogical practice: Thirty-three strategies for dealing with contemporary students.* Lanham, MD: Rowman & Littlefield Education.

Sinagatullin, I. M. (2012). Globalnoye obrazovaniye kak kardinalnaya paradigma novogo veka [Global education as a radical paradigm of the new century]. *Pedagogika, 3,* 14-19.

Solzhenitsyn, A. I. (2002). Shkolnikov uchat po nepravilnim uchebnikam [Schoolchildren are taught with wrong textbooks]. In V. A. Sadovnichiy (Ed.), *Obrazovaniye kotoroye mi modzem poteriat* (pp. 105-111). Moscow: Moscow State University and Institute of Computer Investigation.

Sorokin, P. A. (1991). Tainstvennaya inergiya lubvi [The mysterious energy of love]. *Sociological Studies, 8,* 121-137.

Summer Volunteer Teaching Program. (2007). *Rural Teacher Education Foundation.* Retrieved from http://www.ruralchina.org/site

Teregulov, F. S. (2006). *Geneticheskaya teoriya vselennoy* [The genetic theory of the universe). Ufa, Russia: Gilem.

Tolstoy, L. N. (1989). *Pedagogicheskiye sochineniya* [Pedagogical works], M. I. Kondakov (Ed.), Moscow: Pedagogika.

Utkin, A. I. (2001). *Globalizatsiya: Process i osmisleniye* [Globalization: A process and comprehension]. Moscow: Logos.

Varlamova, T. K. (Ed.). (2003a). Mirovaya entsiklopediya biogrfiy [The world encyclopedia of biographies] (Vol. 10). Moscow: Mir Knigi.

Varlamova, T. K. (Ed.). (2003b). Mirovaya entsiklopediya biogrfiy [The world encyclopedia of biographies] (Vol. 12). Moscow: Mir Knigi.

Virginia's books. (2012). *Hamilton Arts.* Retrieved from http://www. vitginiahamilton.com/virginia-hamilton-books/3/

Volkov, A. (1999). *Etnopedagogika* [Ethnopedagogy]. Moscow: Academa.

Vygotsky, L. S. (1986). *Thought and language.* Cambridge, MA: The MIT Press.

Vygotsky, L. S. (1991). *Pedagogicheskaya psikhologiya* [Pedagogical psychology]. V. V. Davidov (Ed.). Moscow: Pedagogika.

Woodrum, A. (2009). Cultural identity and schooling in rural New Mexico. *Journal of Research in Rural Education, 24*(8). Retrieved from http://jrre.psu.edu/articles/24-8.pdf

World Spanish speaking population statistics. (2009). *SpanisSEO.* Retrieved from http://www.spanishseo.org/resourses/worldwide-spanish-speaking population

# INDEX

## J

## K

## L

## M

## N

## O